THE CURVED TWO-PATCH SYSTEM

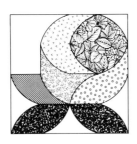

"The immortality of marbles . . . is a vain, small thing compared to the immortality of a flower that blooms and is dead by dusk."

REGINALD FARRER

The Curved Two-Patch System

A Quilter's Exciting Discovery for Creating Pieced Flowers, Foliage and Other Patterns

◇ **JOYCE M. SCHLOTZHAUER**

EPM Publications, Inc.
McLean, Virginia

EPM Publications, Inc., 1003 Turkey Run Road
McLean, Virginia 22101

Printed in the United States of America

Photographs by Myron Miller
Illustrations by Marcia Chadwick
Design by Susan Lehmann

Library of Congress Cataloging in Publication Data

Schlotzhauer, Joyce M.
The curved two-patch system.
Bibliography: p.
Includes indexes.
1. Quilting—Patterns.   2. Patchwork—Patterns.
3. Appliqué—Patterns.   I. Title.
TT835.S34   1982   746.9'7041   82-9666
ISBN 0-914440-56-X

Jacket photograph: Detail of *Floral Collection;* see page 33 for full quilt.

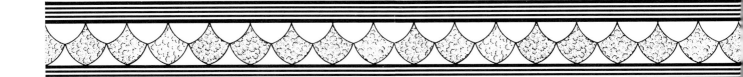

Contents

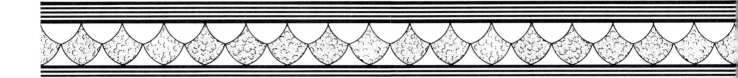

Acknowledgments

My warmest thanks to my husband and our sons, Matt and David. They have endured endless hours of quilt chatter, helped with many technical problems and have often been neglected.

I especially thank Carter Houck for her inspiration. She gave focus to my ideas.

As a longtime fan of Myron Miller's work, I am grateful and appreciative of his photographic talent.

For their help with some of the photographic settings, thanks to the Benjamin Patterson Inn, Mrs. Penrose Hawkes, Nichols' Greenhouse and Mr. and Mrs. William Segar, Jr.

My thanks to Marcia Chadwick for her attention to details while turning my sketches into professional artwork.

Also, I wish to extend my appreciation to those who labored many hours to meet the deadline for photographing quilts and patchwork projects. Thanks to Peg Ames, Romayne Bonk, Eulalia Frenzel, Linda Halpin, Shirley Harkness, Marjory Harris, Louise Hayes, Rose Lovell and Nancy Vineski. An extra thank-you to Nancy Drum, who is the best girl Friday anyone could wish for.

Detail of **Floral Collection** showing hand embroidery. The false eyelet and moiré fabrics are cotton blends.

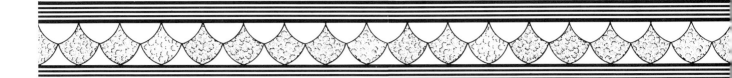

CHAPTER 1

The Taming of the Curved Patch

Perhaps here at the beginning is the best spot to dispel the mystique about use of curves in patchwork before you say, "Oh, oh! Biases!" and put this book back on the shelf. You're a patchworker, aren't you? Then you enjoy the joining of fabric pieces to create new designs. Certainly you sew carefully so that the design is not blurred by sloppy patchwork. If you are a beginner, you have one advantage: No one has instilled the fear in your heart that curved patches are only for the experienced, master quilter. Sometimes such words only intimidate and inhibit the less experienced one, who is anxious to try something new. Although I cannot truthfully say that working with curved patches will produce a quickie quilt, I can say that mastery of—change that to learning—one simple technique can serve you in making any design in this book. That technique is essentially learning *not* to sew in a straight line. Now there's an idea that should have some general appeal!

◇ The Evolution of an Idea

The written advice of quilters—the wise, experienced ones who write books—warns beginners of dangerous curves. This convinced me that the stretchy, bias edges of curved patches are so difficult to handle that I delayed my first attempt until I was bored with straight-line geometrics. So it wasn't until I made my second quilt in 1975 that I decided to try a curved-patch design. With my compass I drew a quarter circle. This made a nice, fat convex patch, but the matching concave one looked ominously skinny. I was daring up to a point, but not up to those long, tapered points. I had to make some concession to my novice status. I knew that a more shallow set of curves would be easier to work with but at the time didn't know how to draw that with a compass. I merely followed the example of past generations and found a plate with a large diameter to trace. The resulting

patches pieced together smoothly. The quilt was successful enough to gain some attention. This pleased me, and I thought someday I would experiment with other arrangements of the two curved patches. That day didn't arrive for several years.

It was the time of the Bicentennial quilt mania, and I caught the excitement. I decided to try a number of straight-line patterns with historic significance for a design to celebrate our country's birthday. The national exposure of that Bicentennial quilt, which was made by members of the Corning Quilter's Guild and myself, gave me enough confidence to continue designing quilts. It wasn't until I was preparing for an exhibit in 1979 and had to produce a plan for the fifteenth quilt that I finally took time to work again with the curved patches.

During trials of twisting and combining the patches, I found a leaf shape. This shape, repeated and rotated around a center point, became daisylike. I think that was my first patched flower. My memory isn't reliable for hanging on to beginnings, but that sounds about right. I do recall that after "discovering" about a half-dozen such flowers, I abandoned the search. There were only two patches per square, and I felt I had exhausted the possibilities. Moreover, some of the original designs weren't merely stylized; they were awkward.

Then Carter Houck of *Lady's Circle Patchwork Quilts* asked if I had a dozen flowers to offer to the quilter who prefers patchwork. I didn't, but by then I knew others could be developed if I concentrated. I studied all the old flower and seed catalogs. Though the brilliantly colored photographs may make a gardener itch for spring, they were of limited help to me. I clipped line drawings of flowers in advertisements. Better. The artists had simplified nature for me. I flipped through the cookie-cutter drawings in children's coloring books, looked over all the greeting card displays and doggedly stared at flowers, nose to petal. It was a matter of interpreting enough of the flower shape to make it recognizable. I rejected more designs then I kept. I went through a number of erasers, and during endless revisions, the erasers went through a number of graph paper sheets. I learned that adding an occasional square or rectangle to the curved patches gave me more flexibility and offered visual relief from the curves. Now the possibilities were limitless. Isn't this often said of combinations of the triangle, square and rectangle? Only the shape of the triangle is different in the Curved Two-Patch System. To make curved patches, I changed the long side of the triangle, the hypotenuse, by bending it a bit, sometimes outward and sometimes inward.

◇ A Plea

My designs were developed to suggest, rather than mimic, flowers. Some are quite realistic, but others are stylized. Complete disregard for patchwork assembly permits an artist to draw botanically accurate specimens; however, to stay within a patchwork system, I have had to take some license with the various blooms. Some may not have their full complement of petals. The shape of the flowers and leaves in nature may be fuller, skinnier, more fringed or more elongated. But nature isn't perfect either. We see flaws and variations among the blooms of a single plant. Also, when we view a flower from a given position, we see it from one angle only. Even a good photograph doesn't reveal all the petals. A leaf may have portions hidden. One flower bent toward the viewer will appear flatter than one seen at an angle.

We allow cartoonists this license. They can distort the human figure, and we enjoy the results. Whoever criticized the bulging forearm muscles of Popeye as unrealistic? Yet we quilters, in attempting a flower in fabric, become unduly demanding that nature be copied faithfully. The graphic artist can have all sorts of license, but is the craftsperson limited to producing patchwork designs under strict laws of propriety?

What I am asking is that you rid yourself of such a mind-set when examining the designs in this book. If one flower is too far from your mental image, look for another. If you like the *Poppy* but think it should be labeled a *Morning Glory*, do so. As I've said, I have taken some license. Now I urge you to do the same.

◇ What This Book Offers to the Quilter

The majority of the patterns in this book are florals, with the addition of some companion designs. Many of the patterns have been available in the past in some form to the appliqué enthusiast, but not to the patchworker. My original intent was to organize the patterns strictly for patching, but I have found that they are easily adapted to appliqué. In regard to this series of designs, the difference between patches and appliqués is the method for making templates. Because the patterns are quite interchangeable, I have included chapter 8 in order to show how to draw the templates for appliqué.

Although we may all be related by our love for quilts, I recognize that our needs and desires differ greatly. For those whose penchant is designing, the individual blocks and borders may suffice. Others may find that the different styles of fully diagrammed quilts best indicate the scope of design possibilities.

To all quilters the Curved Two-Patch System offers three advantages:

1. A basic square unit of two simple curves to produce many designs with:

   the additional use of squares and rectangles; the assembly of blocks in vertical or horizontal rows; the immediate seaming of bias edges in straight-sided units.

2. One set of templates that eliminates the need to enlarge or reduce patterns.

3. One technique to be used for all the designs.

◇ All Patchworkers Can Use This System

I use the term patchworker to include all who work with fabric pieces. Some may never make a bedcover. Some may never do quilting, by hand or by machine. They still start their projects with patches, even those who do appliqué. (Occasionally I feel the lack of a good term for those people. I would use appliqué-ist, if I could spell it sensibly.) More to the point, the book can be used by all—the new enthusiast who may have completed a sampler or the more experienced patchworker whose quilts number in double-digit figures. Only you can assess the degree of complexity that you are willing to undertake.

This is, however, a pattern book, not a basic how-to. I have given techniques that are pertinent to these designs, but I have not tried to teach patchwork principles. With all the quilting publications that are available today, even the novice has access to patchwork references. I have not included a bibliography for special reasons: Some books may be unavailable to you; new quilting publications are appearing with amazing rapidity; and the author's methods and style must suit your needs. Check your local bookstore, the magazine racks and the library for publications on patchwork that discuss such things as yardage estimations, preparation of the quilt sandwich and quilting techniques. With a basic knowledge of patchwork, the beginner can certainly use the curved patches—perhaps starting with a smaller project to gain expertise.

The more experienced will find the complex designs quite manageable.

◇ How to Use the Book

By now you have probably glanced over the floral designs to see what I'm talking about. I hope you will withhold judgment as to their difficulty until your eye becomes adjusted to reading the construction lines within them. Curvilinear patterns can appear particularly difficult, even though they may be easier to assemble than other complex geometric designs. With traditional geometric shapes, we automatically expect a different patch at a point or corner. Thus the mind takes in assembly details at the same time the eye reads the pattern. But the eye naturally follows a flowing line that has no abrupt stops, and a wave of repeated curves presents no visual reminder that "this patch ends here."

To help you break down the designs into the separate patches, this book comes with a Block Marker. This is the inserted, transparent strip on which two different grids are printed. Its purpose is to indicate the number of patches, units and rows within a block or border design. The larger scale of ½″ squares is for the individual block patterns. The ¼″ scale is for the border designs, which are presented in half the scale of the blocks because of the repeats necessary to illustrate at least one corner and part of a border's length.

By overlaying the correct grid on the flower or border, you can divide the design into its square units. If the design underneath this grid has a curve within a square, it means that a convex and concave patch are sewn together to form the square. Chapters 2 and 3 explain the cutting of multiple squares and rectangles that may occur in the flowers or borders. So, of course, a long strip on a side of a patchwork border need not be cut up in small squares.

Several medallion-size flower blocks, which have too many units for the Block Marker to cover, have been printed a second time with a ½″ grid superimposed on the design in order to distinguish the curves, units and rows.

The Block Marker is not used for the diagramed quilts. Each of these has illustrations of the separate modules or blocks with construction lines shown whenever necessary. If the assembly order of the more complex quilts is not obvious, such a diagram is shown with instructions of how to make your own transparent grid to superimpose on the quilt design (p. 81).

Let the Block Marker prove to you that, once the curves are tamed by sewing them into square units, you proceed by following standard patchwork principles. Reading how the system works, as well as the

BLOCK MARKER

For the borders

For the blocks

instructions for the assembly of a sample block, will give you the quickest idea of what you will be doing. At this point don't be too concerned about the discussions of reversals, cautions or even the sewing techniques. That's for referral when you are ready to start work.

For some ideas jump over to chapter 7, "Working With the Designs." Appliqué people should read this chapter in addition to "Freeing the Patterns for Appliqué," chapter 8. Take some time in planning your personal quilt. Quick decisions cut off the creative process. I have known quilters to spend more time shopping for clothes that will be discarded with the passing fashion than they do in choosing a patchwork pattern, which takes months to make but which defies fashion. Try on a few ideas before "buying" a design. An idea that may surface tomorrow can change your quilt from mediocre to memorable. The aim of this book is to help spark such an inspiration.

CHAPTER 2

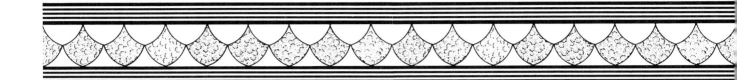

The Curved Two-Patch System

The Basic Unit

All of the patterns of this system are based on the use of two curved patches. One is concave. This means the arc sinks in, as does a cave. Because the word includes "cave" with an *a*, letter this patch A. The other patch is a convex curve. It bows outward as does the letter *b*, so mark it accordingly (fig. 1a and b). Consistent lettering of the patches will help to maintain a mental picture, especially because convex is hardly a household word.

Notice that each patch has three sides. Two sides form a 90° angle and can be cut from the lengthwise and crosswise grain of fabric. In other words, if one straight side of the pattern or template is placed on the fabric parallel to the selvage, the other straight side of the pattern will be parallel to threads across the fabric width. When cut, the patch will have two sides that do not tend to stretch. The third side of the patch forms an arc. This will be a bias cut. Bias cuts stretch. *Easily!*

Figure 2 shows that the bias edges of patches A and B fit together in one seam. Now the two patches become a square with straight-grain sides. The bias edges when sewn together are immediately encased, so there are no further worries about stretching.

These curves are not variations of the *Drunkard's Path* pattern. The arc of that pattern is a quarter circle too small to extend to the diagonal corners. The arc of this system is only gently rounded and easier to sew. (See chapter 3, "How to Draw Templates.")

How the System Works

In developing designs with these curves, I often thought of that childhood pastime of connecting the dots of an invisible design to reveal the outline of a familiar object. The curved-patch system is similar but more disciplined. The dots fall on the intersections of a square grid. Then I allow myself to break one rule. My game allows a curved line across the diagonal to connect two dots. The connect-the-dots

Fig. 1. The curved patches.

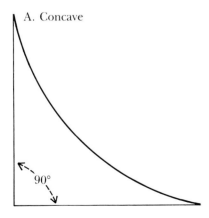
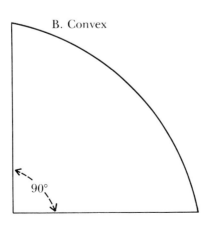

Fig. 2. The square unit.

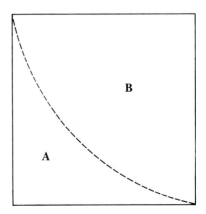

17

game denied us that fun by supplying the curved lines.

The square of A + B is called a unit (to distinguish it from a block) because the designs of this book consist of more than two patches of curves. To make any flower block in this book, the unit is repeated, rotated and occasionally combined with a square that is equal to the unit but cut as one patch. Call it a blank unit. Some designs also include squares and rectangles that are multiples of the unit. The patchwork is that simple.

To introduce the system I have paid strict obedience to three rules:

1. The arc of the A and B patches is constant. The curves in all the patterns are the same, so that only one set of templates is necessary.

2. There is only one seam within a square unit, a bias one. Neither the A or B patch will be cut into more pieces.

3. All vertical and horizontal lines of the patterns represent the straight-grain edges of the units or patches. The square units of all blocks make assembly easy.

At times it is tempting to break one of these disciplines to create a more graceful flower or more realistic leaf, but I have not done so in order to maintain the simple construction of the patterns.

Let me give an example of how advantageous the system can be. If you are a quilt lover, you are probably familiar with the *Clam Shell* pattern (fig. 3a). Quilting books as a rule have cautioned that the pattern is only for the experienced. Wise advice. Look at all those bias edges. Not a straight one in sight! And the next patch will be more of the same! But use the old divide and conquer tactic. If you draw a grid over the pattern, it is easy to see how a similar shell design can be cut using the Curved Two-Patch System (fig. 3b). Of course the scale must be large enough to make it practical to cut the fabric in four patches. There are more pieces to cut, but now you handle just one small bias seam of the design at a time. The arc of these templates is not quite as deep, but if you prefer, the quarter circle of the *Clam Shell* can be substituted. Read about "Combination Patches" in this chapter for another way to cut pieces for the same pattern.

◇ Embroidery Details

I have added an occasional line of embroidery to some of the patterns to give a sense of depth to flower centers, to suggest a bent petal or to give texture to a leaf. These lines, indicated by short dashes, are optional. The patchworker can interpret them in chain stitch, stem stitch, etc.; or they can be omitted. For those who enjoy patchwork but lack time for quilting,

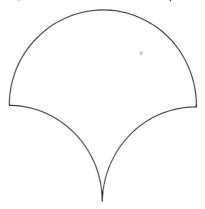

Fig. 3a. Traditional *Clam Shell* pattern.

Fig. 3b. *Clam Shell* in Curved Two-Patch.

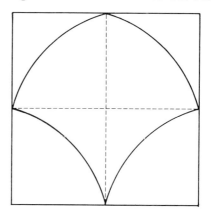

this idea could be translated into tying the quilt's three layers together. Any flower that shows a curved line of embroidery to represent its center would have a perception of depth if a yarn knot depresses that center.

◇ Assembly of Two Sample Blocks

As with conventional patchwork, this assembly system follows common sense, but let's examine some samples to show what to take advantage of and what to avoid. I have chosen two blocks that are representative of the essential details you will encounter. The nine-unit rosebud in figure 4a has eight units of A + B curves and one unit that is a blank. Figure 4b shows a tulip of twelve units. Eight are units of A + B curves; four are blank units. Of these four squares, two can be cut as a double unit, or rectangle.

Here is some good news. As you can readily see from the grid designs, all sewing of these units can be done in either vertical or horizontal rows. There is never a set-in piece!

In this rosebud and tulip, the petals and leaves are formed by repeating and rotating the units.

Fig. 4. Flower blocks with grid overlay reveal their A + B units, blank units and double units.

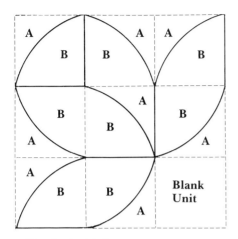

a. Rosebud with leaves.

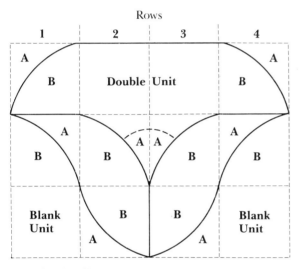

b. Stylized Tulip.

Fig. 5. Avoid difficult block assembly due to cutting segments as patches.

Caution: *The diagram must be followed closely to build the design, with the chosen fabrics cut in the correct curve. Even then it is very easy to pick up two square units and sew the wrong edges together. You need to check often to match the to-be-sewn unit with the one just finished. Chapter 3 suggests a layout sheet as a visual reminder.*

Petals and leaves are usually not complete until you add another unit (or other rows of units); therefore you must realize that adjacent patches often require the same fabric. You will be tempted to combine and cut such patches as one. As a rule, this will complicate the construction of the block. At first glance, the breakdown of the block in figure 5 seems to be logical. Each petal, leaf and background shape is cut as one patch. But how are you going to put the block

back together? It will be a Humpty Dumpty task. If you decide to cut the patches as illustrated, you suddenly discover that you have pattern reversals (see chapter 3, "Combination Templates That Reverse on Fabric"), and the patches now have multiple bias edges. If you surmount this, you sew yourself into a corner, a corner that demands a patch set-in to complete the flower. Although cutting extra patches is hardly an exciting exercise, it does eliminate these complications.

◇ **Combination Patches**

Take heart! There are places where combination patches can be cut. Naturally a row of blank units can be cut as one rectangle (fig. 6a). In other flower designs you can find additional rectangles and squares that are multiples of the unit. There are also some double curves that can sensibly make combination patches. It would be wise, however, to have some practice handling one curve to a unit before choosing to cut two bias edges per patch.

Two sets of double curves occur in the tulip (fig. 6b and c). Each set is a practical choice to cut as one patch because it does not cause a reversal. The set of concave patches calls for the same fabric. If you want to cut the two convex patches as one, you must choose only one fabric for adjacent petals. That will mean that the two outer petals of the tulip are made of the same fabric, because these convex patches form the

19

Fig. 6. Central vertical rows 2 and 3 of the Stylized Tulip block. The incomplete petals are shaded.

Combined rows

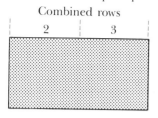

a. Double unit cut as one rectangular patch.

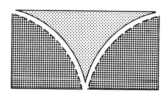

b. Double concave patch with convex patches to form double unit.

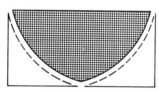

c. Double convex patch can be cut if the two outside petals are of the same fabric.

Fig. 7. Modules of the rosebud showing combination patches for 2 leaves and 1 petal.

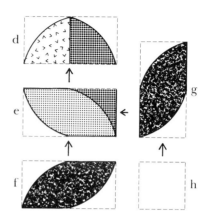

base of both petals. Then with the addition of a curved patch at either end of the combinations, a double unit (or rectangle of three patches) is formed.

Before cutting combination patches, consider whether to sew the tulip vertically or horizontally. The rows can be joined horizontally with no set-in patches. You have the option to complete the center as shown and add the outside units as vertical rows.

The rosebud (fig. 7) has a different set of curves. Let's suppose you choose to make an entire quilt of this rosebud block. (See *Rosebud Wreath* in chapter 6.) With many leaves to cut, you may want to make a combination template for cutting patches, even though it involves pattern reversals. Consider cutting each leaf as one patch made up of two B (convex) curves. You can do this because there is no fabric change within a leaf. (Note that the same can be done with one petal.) Then by adding a concave patch at either end of the leaf, you sew a double unit. (See fig. 7f and g.)

These combination units change the construction of the block, but the five modules offer another easy assembly order. Double units e and f are sewn to the completed d. (Module d has four patches because of fabric changes for two petals.) Then double unit g is sewn to the blank square h. This row can then be joined to d, e, f to complete the block. The block was not sewn in all vertical or horizontal rows, but an equally simple sewing order was found.

I leave it to you to find other combination patches

in the individual blocks. Most, except the ones already noted, will cause reversals. Do you choose the reversals rather than cutting separate patches? Common sense, and perhaps a bit of self-confidence, will guide you in deciding. Before you start cutting fabric, here's a reminder:

Combination templates can be used when the construction of the block is not affected or when another assembly order has been found. If cutting double patches means others must be set in, you have complicated the pattern needlessly.

Once again, all patterns can be joined in vertical or horizontal rows, but they don't have to be. In the rosebud block, to cut fewer patches, another easy joining order was found.

This overall, quick look at the system is to give you enough details to believe that it works. Having read through sample block assemblies in this chapter, you are better qualified to judge the simplicity or complexity of the designs.

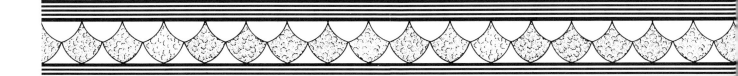

CHAPTER 3

Techniques and Templates

There seems to be a common distaste for enlarging or reducing patterns. This is not often stated, but I notice quilters seek patterns of a given size. To make your work easier, a sheet of templates for the curves and corresponding blank squares is provided at the end of this chapter. These will eliminate the need to redraw the blocks to obtain templates in the size desired.

◇ Template Size Determines Block Measurement

Each block design is labeled with the number of units across and down. This does *not* refer to actual size in inches. You are going to decide that. You patchworkers who are more accustomed to measurements in centimeters will find this system useful too, if you draw the templates on the metric scale. The method for drawing any size template is explained in the following section.

First you must decide the size of quilt block with which you want to work. Then choose the template size according to the number of square units of the block.

Let's say you want two flowers in 8″ blocks and have chosen the *Posy* as one. Use the Block Marker as an overlay to divide the pattern into its square units. Figure 8a shows the *Posy* has four units across and down; therefore you use the 2″ templates. For the second flower, you would like the *Poppy* (fig. 8b), but it looks so small. The 2″ templates would make a *Poppy* 4″ x 4″. You would rather it equaled the size of the *Posy*. You don't have to use higher math to see that each unit of the *Poppy* must be 4″ to make an 8″ block, as shown in figure 8c. There is no need to draw an enlarged block for new templates. Just pick up the 4″ ones. This also works in reverse to scale the *Posy* down to a 4″ *Poppy* block; but you need to be a fan of miniature patchwork, for the units of the *Posy* would

Fig. 8. Diagrams show relative size of blocks. Units can be in inches or centimeters.

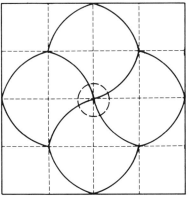

a. *Posy:* 4 units by 4 units.

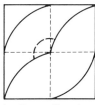

b. *Poppy:* 2 units by 2 units.

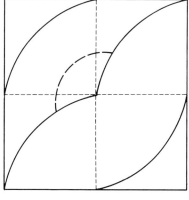

c. *Poppy* equaling *Posy*. Use templates twice as large as those needed in figure 8b.

be 1″ squares. In other words, all the block designs are given in the same scale to show their relative sizes. That relationship can be changed by choice of template size. By way of summary, here is an equation:

Desired block size in inches (or centimeters)
÷ Number of units (across or down)
= Size of templates in inches (or centimeters)

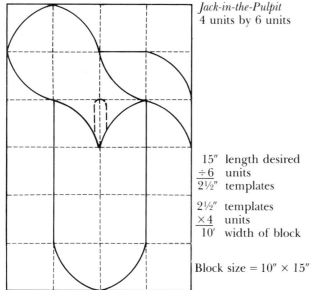

Jack-in-the-Pulpit
4 units by 6 units

$$\begin{array}{rl} 15'' & \text{length desired} \\ \div 6 & \text{units} \\ \hline 2\frac{1}{2}'' & \text{templates} \end{array}$$

$$\begin{array}{rl} 2\frac{1}{2}'' & \text{templates} \\ \times 4 & \text{units} \\ \hline 10' & \text{width of block} \end{array}$$

Block size = 10″ × 15″

Fig. 9. Determining size of templates for rectangular design.

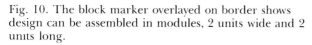

Fig. 11. Method for drawing concave and convex curves to any size. Substitute desired template size for the 2¼″ square.

Fig. 10. The block marker overlayed on border shows design can be assembled in modules, 2 units wide and 2 units long.

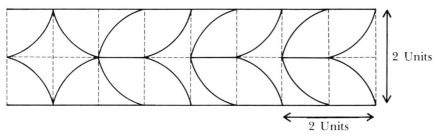

2 Units

2 Units

Use the same equation for rectangular blocks. Because you will probably be more concerned with the length of the block, divide by that number of units. Your width will then be equal to the size of the templates times the number of units across. In case words get in the way of the obvious, see figure 9.

The equation works for the border designs also. Figure 10 shows a portion of the *Spray of Leaves* border. Placing the Block Marker over the border design reveals units in two rows. How long do you want each leaf? How tall is the diamond? Determining these measurements helps to scale the border. The width of the border is two units. For a border 8″ wide, use 4″ templates. If the length of your border can be 88″, the double units will be repeated 11 times. This odd number allows for a centered diamond, four leaf blocks to either side and corner diamonds.

◇ **How to Draw Templates**

The sheet of templates for tracing offers the most

commonly called-for sizes. Should you need an in-between size, figure 11 illustrates the method for obtaining any size template in inches or in centimeters. I have used 2¼″ as the desired square unit for this drawing.

1. Draw a 2¼″ square on graph paper. (Professional quality paper, such as vellum, is the most accurate.)

2. Draw a vertical line (C) ¾″ outside the square, parallel to a side and extended past a corner of the square.

3. Draw a second line (D) perpendicular to line C. This is also ¾″ outside the square. Extend this line to intersect with line C at point E.

4. Place the pivot point of the compass at point E.

5. Spread the pencil point of the compass to point F.

6. Swing an arc downward to the diagonal corner, point G.

Fig. 12. Leaf drawn with different arcs.

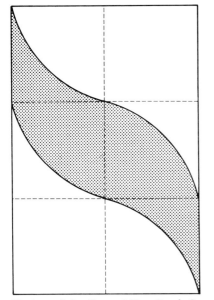

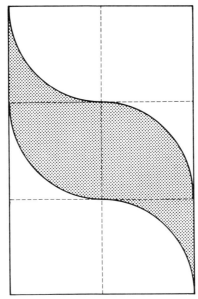

X. Arc of the Curved Two-Patch System.

Y. Arc of a quarter circle.

The square is now divided into concave (A) and convex (B) curves with sides measuring 2¼". Whatever the size of template needed, substitute your dimensions for the size of the square unit and then proceed as above to find the arc used for the patterns of this book. For those who use the metric system, substituting 2 cm for the ¾" distance will give almost the same arc. To make the arc slightly rounder, draw the intersecting lines 1.5 cm outside the square.

You may want to experiment with drawing a curve tailored to you. To do this, place the compass point anywhere along the diagonal line H in figure 11. The closer that point is to the corner of the square, the deeper the arc. Choosing a more distant placement for the compass point flattens the arc.

I have chosen the ¾" distance from the square to draw the intersecting lines. It is possible, of course, to use a quarter circle for the A and B curves by placing the compass point in a corner of the square, but I wanted a more shallow arc that permits the two curved patches to be sewn with ease. Also, I have found that some of the designs with reverse curves—those that bow out and in again—appear more relaxed or natural than the deep S-curve made by quarter circles. As an example, figure 12 shows the curves of a leaf drawn with different arcs. In figure 13, three different arcs are drawn in one square to illustrate the gentleness of this system's curved patches.

For simplicity in drafting the curves, I have used the same compass setting for all the templates. The

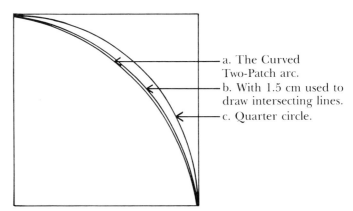

a. The Curved Two-Patch arc.
b. With 1.5 cm used to draw intersecting lines.
c. Quarter circle.

Fig. 13. Arcs by three measurements.

change in the arc of the template sizes used most often is negligible; however, a 1″ template has a somewhat flatter arc. Refer to the photo of the *Bell Pull* by Eulalia Frenzel, page 71, to see appliqué made with a 1″ template that uses this system's arc. Among the photographed patchwork projects, the smallest patches were used for the pieced box. For this, Nancy Vineski chose 1″ templates (page 36). All photographed quilts and smaller projects were made with the templates that this book provides. However, if you work with small appliqué pieces or miniature patchwork, you may want to move the compass point closer to the square's corner to strike a deeper arc.

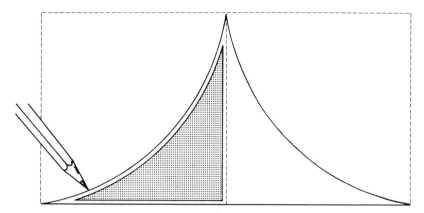

Fig. 14. To make a combination template (A + A), draw the units first. This establishes a straight line for the base.

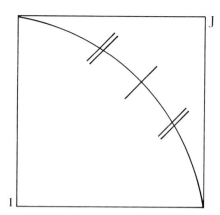

Fig. 15. Center match marks and side match marks for larger templates.

The quilt design of your choice may need patterns for the A and B curves and the square; at the same time, it may give you the option of using combination templates. To draw these combinations, first cut the A and B patterns. Then, following the example of figure 14, draw the outline of the units into which the combination fits. Trace the curves of the A and B patterns to complete the desired combination.

◇ Match Marks and Seam-Reminder Marks

On the template sheet at the end of this chapter, notice the line that bisects the arc. Don't forget to copy this short line on your templates. This I call a match mark. It indicates the center of each curve and is an aid in matching the two curved patches when you start pinning. Match marks serve the patchworker as notches do the seamstress. Later you'll be happy to have them marked in the seam allowance of the patches when you see that the two curves do not line up to each other as neatly as square patches.

If you are making your own templates, draw the square unit and, as previously described, draw the arc for the A and B curves. *Before* cutting apart the square for the two curved patches, place a ruler diagonally across the unit so that it bisects the arc (points I and J in fig. 15). Draw a short line across the arc so that both A and B patches will have their centers matched. If your square unit is small, the center mark is sufficient. For larger templates, make another such mark on either side of, and parallel to, the center one. If your choice of patterns calls for combination templates, draw the same match marks on any edge that has a curve. It is also a help on these combination templates to draw a seam-reminder mark—an indication of an eliminated seam (fig. 16). This reference mark aids in matching two rows of units when some squares are patched and others skip a seam.

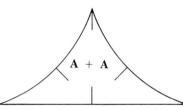

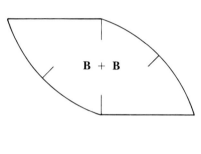

Fig. 16. Combination templates show match marks and seam reminders.

You will become aware of the fine points of the concave curve when you cut the templates. These will be difficult to control if you use cardboard or sandpaper. A fairly stiff plastic that can still be cut is a good choice for the templates. Precise patchwork depends upon the accuracy with which you mark patches. Precise marking, in turn, depends upon templates with tapered points that don't yield or wear away.

◇ Combination Templates That Reverse on Fabric

In chapter 2, "Assembly of Two Sample Blocks," I discussed the practicality of cutting some curved patches as combinations. Some combined curves, however, call for the reversal (or flipping over) of the template. In a block, you will often find sets of these combination curves that are mirror images.

Fig. 17. Templates must be reversed (flipped over). Leaves are mirror images.

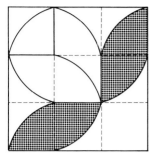

a. Leaf at bottom of rosebud block.

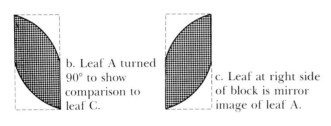

b. Leaf A turned 90° to show comparison to leaf C.

c. Leaf at right side of block is mirror image of leaf A.

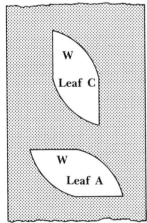

d. Templates with wrong side up. Fabric with wrong side up.

Let's use the rosebud block again to demonstrate what you must do (fig. 17). First, that innocent-appearing combination of two convex curves for a whole leaf must be reversed to mark the patch on the wrong side of the fabric. To make the template, use plastic or cardboard so you can mark the right and wrong sides. (Unfortunately, sandpaper has only one side that can be marked.) Cut the template exactly the same as the leaf in the pattern. Mark this the right

side. Turn the template over and mark this as the wrong side. The leaf at the bottom of the rosebud is shown in figure 17a. The placement of the combination template in figure 17d shows both the wrong side of the fabric and the template facing up.

Second, notice that the two leaves are mirror images. In figure 17b, the leaf from the bottom of the rosebud is drawn vertically. This illustrates that the leaf is not the same as leaf C. No matter how many directions it's turned, it remains different. Instead of trying to remember how to use the template for a reversed leaf, I advise you to make a new template for leaf C that is the reverse of leaf A. You must also turn over this template to mark patches, as in figure 17d. Along with marking the right and wrong sides of the templates, it may be helpful to mark a reminder on the right sides, *reverse to cut*. Then do so without thinking about it. It will seem that you are marking the leaves wrong, but when the cut patches are turned to their right sides, the leaves are miraculously the same as in the pattern.

This process is one of those things that the novice must try before being convinced. I still double check myself as if I can't believe it. You may be one of the experienced patchworkers who find such details elementary, but I bet you're smiling ruefully to yourself remembering a few wasted cuts. If all this reversal business seems just too much to handle, don't make this combination template. You will have more patches to mark and cut, but you won't waste fabric. Best of all, the single curves can turn in any direction if your material is not directional.

◇ Placement of Templates on Directional Fabric

The cutting of patches, single or multiple, entails some attention to the placement of the templates on fabric. The two curved patches turn in any direction with no reversals, unless directional fabric is chosen. If you are a collector of calico prints, there should be no problem. If you choose a solid color fabric, you should check to see if changing direction of the grain will cause a shading of the color. Chintz and cotton sateen are two examples of materials in which the shade of a horizontally grained patch laid next to a vertically grained one will be noticeably different. To check, simply fold over a sizeable corner of your solid color fabric so that both grains of the right side of the material overlap. Walk around the fabric so that you look at it in changing light. If you do not detect any color variation, you can cut the curved patches in any direction and join them.

I have found, however, that many solid color cottons and blends, particularly the deeper tones, appear quite different when patches of vertical and

Fig. 18. Avoid shading of vertical and horizontal grains of solid color fabrics.

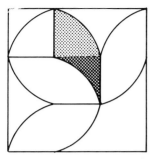

a. Avoid cutting one patch of petal on different grain.

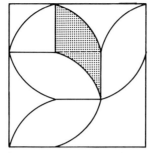

b. Correct: Both patches of the petal are cut from same fabric grain. Reverse templates on directional fabric.

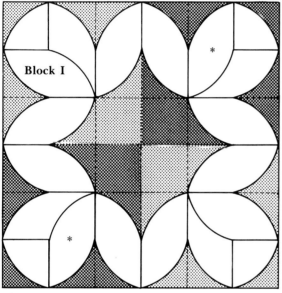

c. *Caution:* The 90° rotation of block I to form a square of 4 blocks can cause shading of fabric grains. Only blocks in diagonal corners (180° rotation) appear identical.

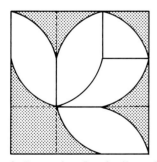

d. Correction for shading of background fabric:
1. Turn the pattern to match a block with asterisk (18c*).
2. Mark this block II.
3. Cut background patches according to their positions in block II.
4. Assemble block II for diagonal corners (18c*).

horizontal grain are juxtaposed. Before cutting patches you should plan the placement of templates on such fabrics to avoid blotches within a flower or leaf. In nature we may have to put up with imperfections, but blotchiness in a patchwork flower wouldn't even look like a natural disease.

A solid color fabric that shades with a change of grain is equivalent to a directional fabric. This necessitates reversing the A and B templates when marking the patches. To illustrate, I have shown one petal of the rosebud in figure 18a that has two patches of a solid color fabric. Because one patch appears darker than the other, the patches don't blend together to make a realistic petal. The result is distracting. Perhaps the curved patches were cut on different grains (one on the vertical, the other on the horizontal). However, it is more probable that one template was not reversed on the directional fabric. Then the patch had to be rotated 90° for block assembly. Figure 18b shows the same petal with both patches cut on the same grain.

The same shading phenomenon can occur with solid color fabrics for backgrounds because quilt blocks are constantly rotated 90°. In a repeated block quilt, such as the *Rosebud Wreath*, it would seem natural to cut patches for all blocks like block I (fig. 18c) because it appears to rotate. It's easy to forget that the grain of the background fabric also rotates. Will your solid color background reflect that change of grain direction? If so, then make it a rule to rotate the pattern first, consider this block II, and cut the patches in the same direction that they will occur in the assembled quilt. With the *Rosebud Wreath*, make half the blocks like block II (fig. 18d) to solve the problem. When four blocks are assembled, the identical ones are in diagonal corners.

I have talked only about avoiding the shading effect of the two fabric grains. There are places where the deliberate combination of the horizontal and vertical fabric grains can be advantageous. This combination of fabric grains would subtly shade adjacent petals or leaves. Remember this when you have difficulty finding the third or fourth fabric for the more complex flowers.

Should some unwanted shading show only after completion of the quilt top, my advice is to add a lot of quilting. By breaking up the surface with the hills and valleys of quilting lines, particularly lines in opposite directions, you may find that light can no longer play on enough flat surface to show the change of grain line. Or hope that quilt historians will find your casual rotation of fabric grain as charming as the old Amish quilts that display such nonchalance.

26

WRONG SIDE OF FABRIC

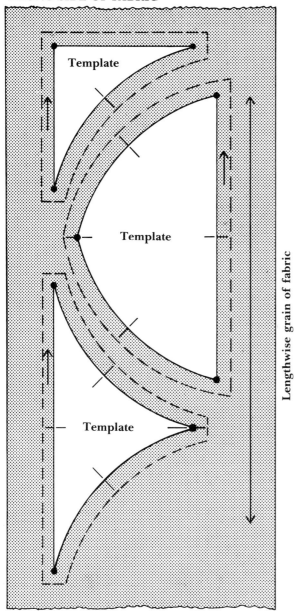

Fig. 19. Patches marked with information in seam allowances. Dash lines indicate seam allowances.

Lengthwise grain of fabric

1. The match marks of the curves.
2. The seam reminders on combination templates.
3. A dash or arrow to indicate the straight grain.

This third addition of information will be helpful in matching grains to prevent unwanted shading of solid color patches.

◇ Handling the Curved Patches

A word about the handling of those bias edges—*don't!* You should stack them and leave them. It would be interesting to speculate why patchworkers unconsciously pat, smooth and straighten piles of patches, but curved edges survive better without such fondling. The ability of a bias to give is an advantage you want to reserve for fitting the patches together.

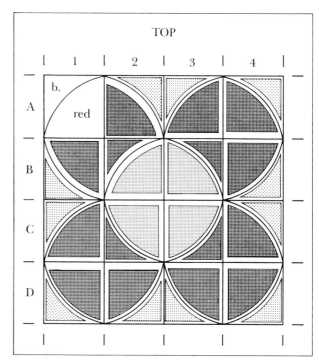

Fig. 20. Layout sheet with patches placed in respective squares. Patches for unit A-1 are removed to reveal direction of curve and color coding.

◇ Marking Fabric Patches With the Templates

You can maintain good corners when marking patches if you start by making dots to indicate each corner or point before running a pencil line around the template. Fabric gives under the pressure of a pencil, and corners can be pulled or distorted. With a dot in the corner first, you know just how far to extend the line. This marking is the sewing line. Add the usual ¼″ seam allowance to all sides and use that space for write-in information (fig. 19):

◇ Layout Sheet for Organizing Patches

Even though all the designs are developed by the same techniques, some are visually more complex than others because of various combinations of A + B units. The patterns can be confusing. As mentioned earlier, assembly demands close attention to the master pattern.

In an effort to cut a big project down to size and to organize it, I recommend that you make a layout sheet. Paper will do; flannel or felt is better because

27

fabric sticks to it. Cut this somewhat larger than your block design so that margins are available for write-in information (fig. 20). On this sheet, draw, with a felt-tip pen, a rough grid of squares equal to the number of units in your block. Make the squares ½" larger than the pattern to accommodate the seam allowances of the patches. This is merely a visual reminder, so you needn't worry about exact measurements. In the margins, mark the horizontal rows with letters and the vertical rows with numbers. (Vice versa works just as well.) Roughly draw each patch in its proper square, such as unit A-1. You can color code the layout sheet for further information. If the pattern is symmetrical, as in the example (fig. 20), it may also be of help to mark the top of the design on the layout sheet to prevent accidental rotation of the block. Cut the patches for each unit and place them on the layout sheet in the correct direction.

When you are ready to sew, remove only one A + B unit at a time, sew and replace it with the direction of the curve matching your drawn diagram. After an interruption or distraction, you won't absentmindedly pick up two square units and sew the wrong edges together.

The layout sheet can also be adapted for portable patchwork. For carrying, choose flannel so you can pin the patches to it. Cut the sheet twice as long as your pattern and use the extra to fold over and protect the patches.

'When I was piecing *Floral Collection*, shown on the front cover, I used a similar idea. The patched nosegay, in regards to assembly, is one mammoth patchwork block. I sewed together strips of heavy flannel for a layout sheet. I marked a grid on the sheet and tacked it to a cork wall in our basement. Having the diagram vertical was helpful when I wanted to shift fabrics until I was happy with the arrangement. One day I realized that I would be isolated in the basement during the entire patching of the quilt! It certainly wasn't practical to take all those patches off the wall to rearrange elsewhere. The problem was solved by cutting and coding extra flannel strips for single half rows. I marked squares on the strips and lettered them to match the original layout sheet. Then each time I removed a half row of patches from the wall to pin to the strip, I also pinned to it a paper note recording the row number. After sewing the patches together, I returned the half row to the flannel sheet and used the strip for the patches of the next row. At times I used several of these portable strips while I was traveling.

◇ Techniques for Sewing the Curved Patches

It's not that the technique for sewing curves differs much from that of typical patchwork; it's just more

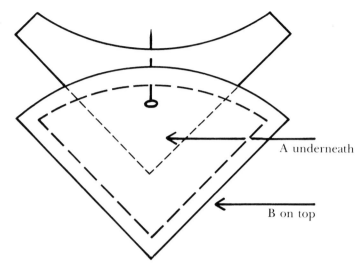

Fig. 21. Pin A and B patches with right sides together. Pins should pierce and be perpendicular to seam lines.

exacting. With straight-edged piecing, the two fabric patches line up naturally; not much pinning is required to hold them. Once you start to sew along a straight line, the needle tends to continue on that line. With curves you are going to do what looks impossible.

Start by holding the concave patch with the right side of the fabric up. Place the convex patch on top, right side down (fig. 21). The idea is to fit these two curves into a happy match. At this point they look like a warring couple, standing back to back and headed in opposite directions. Match up the centers first and, with a pin, pierce the seam line at the match mark. Check on the underneath patch to see that the pin went through that seam line at the center match mark. I usually place a pin in each corner next to start moving the curves together. Halve the distance between the corner and center and pin again. On larger patches, there will be another match mark here. Continue in this manner to pin the two curves together. I use lots of pins and leave no more than a ½" between them, usually less. It's like sticking a soap bubble to break it into two small bubbles, then into four bubbles and so forth. Finally the bubbles of the bias edges are so small that your stitches will hold the patches in alignment. Precision pinning makes hand sewing easier. Adjust the number of pins according to the size of the templates and your expertise in sewing a smooth curve.

To hand sew the pinned unit, start with a knot at the corner (of the seam line) and a backstitch. Proceed with only three or four stitches and check the back. It's the extreme corners that will seem particularly stubborn. If your needle on the last stitch has just started off the line, bring it back with a backstitch.

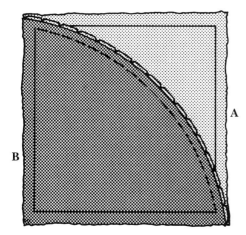

Fig. 22. Sewn unit with patch A clipped. Darker fabric of patch B trimmed.

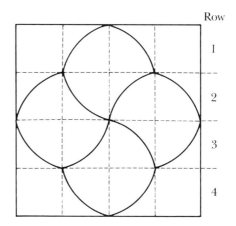

Row
1
2
3
4

Fig. 23a. Points of curved seam must be tapered at corners of units. Center of *Posy* has points of 8 patches to match.

This will help strengthen your work, too. Insistence on filling the needle with stitches on each pass will more than likely send you off the seam line of the A patch underneath. Use backstitches at the end of the seam, but leave the seam allowances free to be turned in either direction.

Clip the A curve once the unit is sewn, but not so deeply as to endanger the seam. The purpose is to allow the seam allowance to be pressed toward the A patch, a practice usually recommended (fig. 22). I have found times when it was preferable to turn the seam allowance toward the B patch, either because of color or type of fabric, or the placement of a future quilting line. In that case, I clip the small bubbles in the edge of the B curve to allow the fabric to move together and overlap. To keep all options open, I have also clipped both seam allowances. Check to see if a dark-colored fabric shows through a light-colored one when the allowance is turned toward the light one. Trim the edge if necessary (fig. 22).

Machine stitching of the A + B unit can be done if your templates are large enough. With 3″ patches, Romayne Bonk pieced *Dutch Bulbs* entirely by machine. With the 1¾″ patches of *Floral Collection*, I found that preparing for machine stitching has an advantage. This preparation includes a line of machine stay-stitching inside the seam allowance of the A curve (but very close to the seam line) and then the clipping of the curve up to the line of stay-stitching. When it's time to pin the unit, the A curve is quite amenable. No worry about stretching the bias because it is stay-stitched, and the clipping helps the adjustment of the curves. But even with machine stitching, I use many pins to hold the patches and remove each as the machine approaches it. Again, it is a good idea to keep the seam allowances free.

Sewing the A and B patches into units is not difficult by hand or machine. The basic idea is to sew a smooth curve and to taper the seam to points. This is critical when the curves of two different units meet within a row. For an example, refer to figure 23a. In row 1 of the *Posy*, the curved seams of two units touch to define the edge of a petal. Tapered curves are even more important when you join rows of curved units, such as rows 2 and 3 of the *Posy*. With precise patching, the curves will flow across an unobtrusive seam.

Piece the center of the *Posy* in the same manner as a traditional eight-pointed star pattern, because there are eight patches that must meet at a center point. For hand sewing of rows 2 and 3, begin the seam from the outside edge of the block. When you reach the center, lift the seam allowance of each patch and pass the needle through the point of the corresponding patch on the opposite side of the seam. Repeat this procedure across the center of the design and then continue sewing the seam in normal fashion. This will insure matching points. To machine sew the seam, use this hand-sewing method to tack the center points before proceeding. The sewing machine will not like the bulk of the many seams that must be crossed. If rows 2 and 3 are merely pinned, some of the points will be shoved to the side. There is no objection to having the allowances sewn down after these points are matched satisfactorily.

The *Posy* with its eight points is one of the more complicated examples. Your choice of pattern may be simpler, such as the leaf in figure 23b. There are fewer patches to match in the center of rows 1 and 2, but they must meet for the outline of the leaf to be distinct. If yours look like the blurred one of figure 23c, it may be due to the way you marked the patches. Does the curved seam end at the exact corners of the

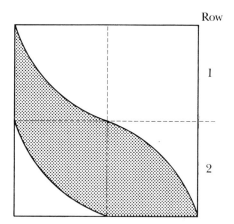

Fig. 23b. The tapered points of the curved patches must meet when two rows are assembled.

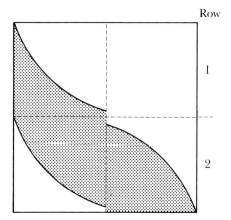

Fig. 23c. Blurred leaf image due to poor tapering of curved patches.

Fig. 24. Use of blocking cloth.

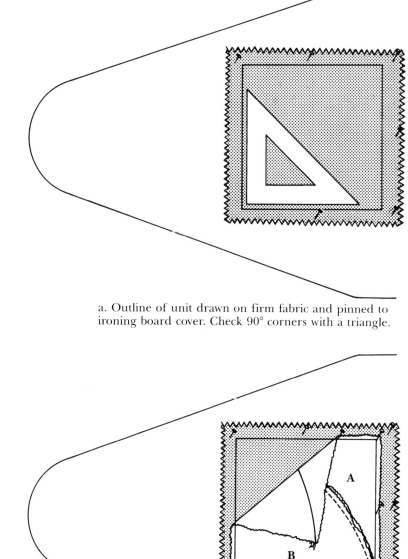

a. Outline of unit drawn on firm fabric and pinned to ironing board cover. Check 90° corners with a triangle.

b. Pin the sewn unit (wrong side up) with seam line matched to outline drawn on the blocking cloth.

sewn unit? Perhaps the last stitch in the curved seam does not meet the seam line that crosses it. As the work on your quilt progresses, you will be happier if you insisted on precision from the beginning. You also will want to avoid ripping stitches out of stretchy bias edges.

◇ The Use of a Blocking Cloth

The pressing of patchwork seams can also be a special technique. I block seams by using a special cloth. To make a blocking cloth, choose a very firm—and that is the operative word here—piece of fabric on which to draw the outline of the square unit. This outline is equivalent to the seam lines of a unit. Leave an ample

margin around the outline for the placement of pins, and cut. Pin this cloth to a padded ironing board cover with the outline of the unit right side up (fig. 24a). On top of this, with the right side down, place your sewn A + B unit. Pin through the seam lines of the sewn unit, through the outline of the blocking cloth and into the ironing board cover (fig. 24b). Do this first at the corners. Then add as many pins as

30

necessary. Now press the seam allowance toward the A patch. (Later when the entire block is pressed, you may want to change the direction in which some seams are pressed.) When this unit is pressed, you know the dimensions are exact and the corners square.

Patchwork seams in a block work like an accordian. Without blocking, the pressed patchwork can be smaller than requirements because of seams rolling over, or it can be larger or out-of-square because of an overzealous hand on the iron. This blocking is a logical and easy thing to do. It also gives me a sense of confidence that I am preventing a future disappointment. Some time ago I read that too much pressing can stretch fabric. Exactly my point! Without blocking, how are you to know if the unit or quilt block is exactly the measurements called for or that the corners are true? I think it's foolhardy to assume that if patches fit together, everything will turn out fine. I will back off a bit: After you've had some experience with successful units and rows of them, you may find that you can delay the pressing until an entire quilt block is finished. Then size your blocking cloth to that measurement.

There is a danger of overemphasizing technique to the point of dampening enthusiasm. The details of this chapter are only helpers to get you started. You may later develop methods that work better for you.

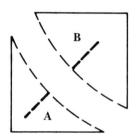

Example of a square unit cut into the A and B templates showing match marks.

THE TEMPLATES

This is a series of seven template sizes. The dash line, which divides each square into the A and B templates, is the arc of the Curved Two-Patch System. The short dashes across the arcs are aids in matching the A and B patches. Choose the square that will size your block design to the desired dimension (see chapter 3, "Template Size Determines Block Measurement"). Because most of the designs require three templates, trace and transfer to template material the square as well as A and B. Cut the set of templates and check for accuracy. A and B must fit together and be equal to the square.

4″

3½″

3″

2½″

2″

1½″

1″

31

Climbing Vine, 22″ x 32″, designed and made by Rose Lovell. Flower centers are crewel turkey-work. Some petals and leaves are stuffed.

32

Floral Collection, 55″ x 66″, was designed and made by the author. The fabrics are cottons and blends, and cotton batiste innerlining. Patchwork was done by hand and machine; embroidery and quilting, by hand.

Blue Hearts, 45″ x 55″, by Eulalia Frenzel, author's design. An appliquéd version of the *Pennsylvania Dutch Crib Quilt.* All appliqué and quilting by hand.

Power of the Pansy, 36″ x 36″, made by Susan Croft, designed by Joyce Schlotzhauer. All cotton fabrics, hand-pieced and hand-quilted.

Dried Arrangement, 80″ x 95″, made with cottons and blends by Shirley Harkness and Marjory Harris. Piecing, embroidery and quilting by hand. Author's design.

Tiger Lily box designed and made by Nancy Vineski.
The one-inch patches were machine-pieced.

Wild Rose pillow made by Eulalia Frenzel with hand-appliqué and hand-quilting. Author's design.

CHAPTER 4

The Flower Blocks

The universal love of flowers is evident in every art and craft. In quilting, however, graceful floral patterns have been developed for only one facet of the craft, appliqué. The few geometric flower designs that exist lack the softness of nature even though piecing with curves is fairly common. I hope that these flower blocks will break through that limitation to add another dimension to patchwork.

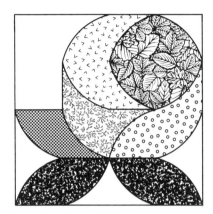

Opening Rose #1 4 x 4 units

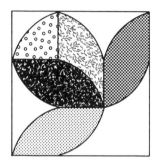

Rosebud 3 x 3 units

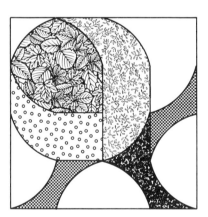

Opening Rose #2 4 x 4 units

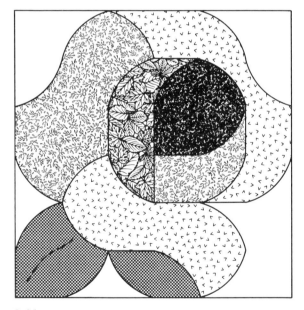

Cabbage Rose 6 x 6 units

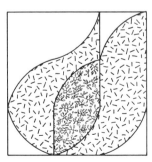

Blossom Bud 3 x 3 units

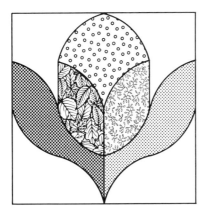

Formal Bud 4 x 4 units

Painted Daisy 6 x 6 units

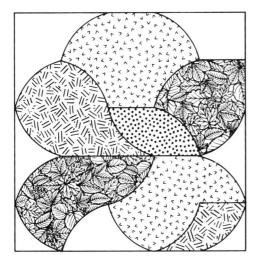

Wild Rose 5 x 5 units

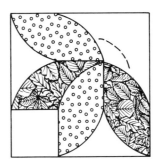

Daisy in Profile 3 x 3 units

Bud in the Breeze 5 x 5 units

Bursting Bud 4 x 3 units

Black-eyed Susan 6 x 6 units

Daisies Never Tell 4 x 4 units

Morning Glory 4 x 4 units

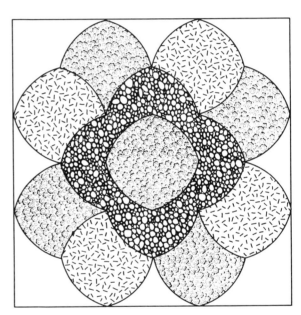

Anemone 6 x 6 units

Poppy #1 2 x 2 units

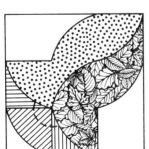

Bluebonnet
3 x 3 units

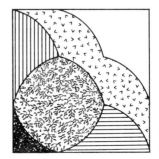

Poppy #2
3 x 3 units

41

Periwinkle 6 x 6 units

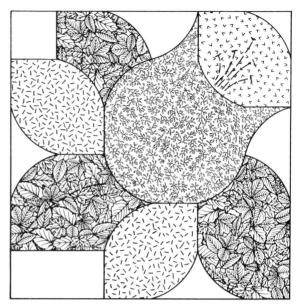

Daffodil 6 x 6 units

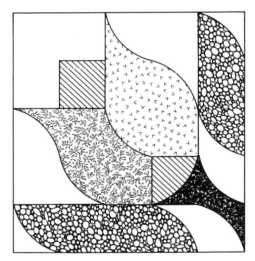

Tulip #1 5 x 5 units

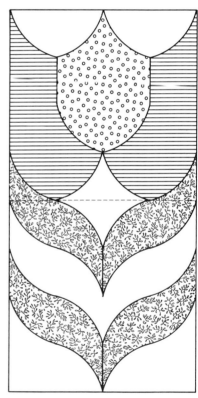

Tulip #2 with leaf block
4 x 4 units each

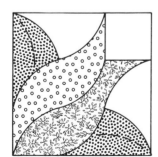

Tulip #3
3 x 3 units

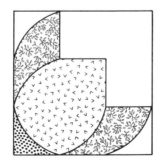

Tulip #4
3 x 3 units

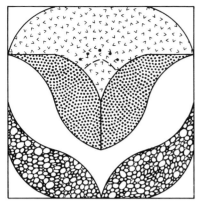 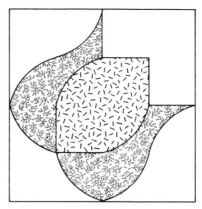 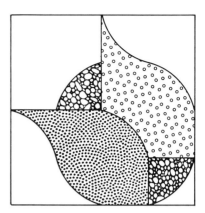

Tulip #5 4 x 4 units   **Tulip #6** 4 x 4 units   **Tulip #7** 4 x 4 units

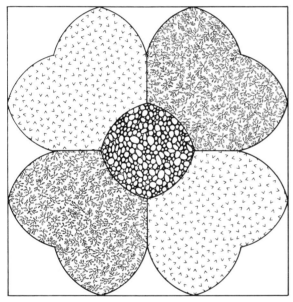

Sundrop 6 x 6 units

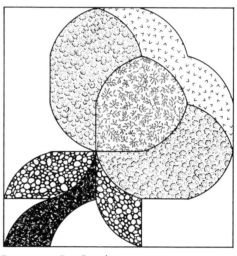

Buttercup 5 x 5 units

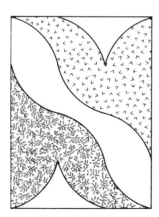

Waltz of the Tulips
3 x 4 units

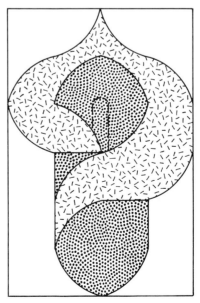

Calla Lily 4 x 6 units

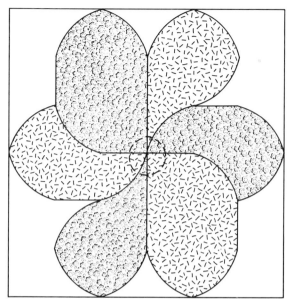

Cosmos 6 x 6 units

Lady Slipper 5 x 6 units

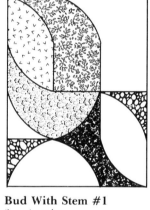

Bud With Stem #1
3 x 4 units

Bud With Stem #2
3 x 4 units

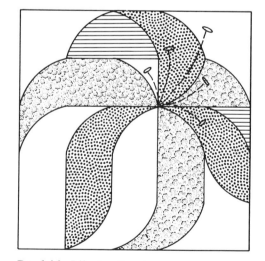

Roadside Lily 5 x 5 units

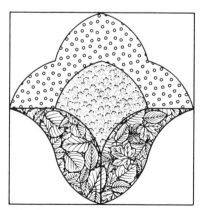

Stylized Lily #1   4 x 4 units

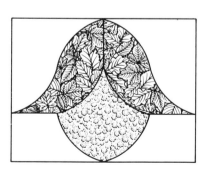

Stylized Lily #2   4 x 3 units

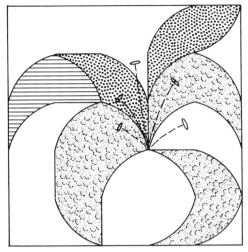

Tiger Lily 5 x 5 units

Lily Bud and Leaves 5 x 5 units

Lily Bud
3 x 3 units

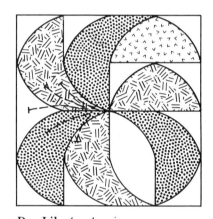

Day Lily 4 x 4 units

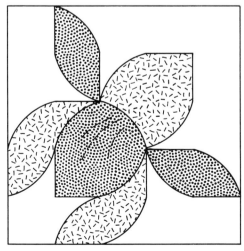

Chinese Orchid 5 x 5 units

Orchid 5 x 5 units

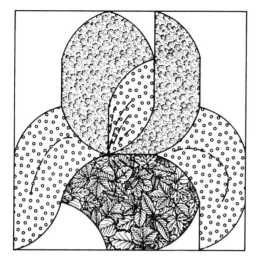

Iris 5 x 5 units

Iris Bud 5 x 5 units

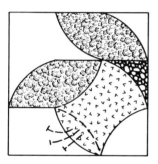

Trumpet Vine 3 x 3 units

Spring Bulb 4 x 4 units

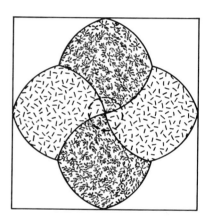

Posy 4 x 4 units

Starflower 6 x 6 units

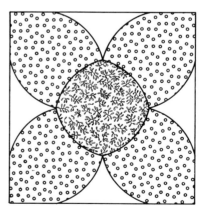

Bluet 4 x 4 units

Violet 6 x 6 units

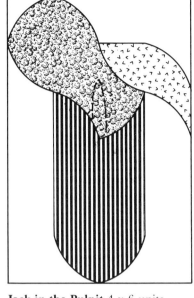

Jack-in-the-Pulpit 4 x 6 units

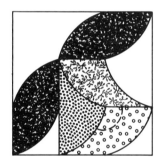

Bell Blossom 3 x 3 units

Crocus #2 6 x 6 units

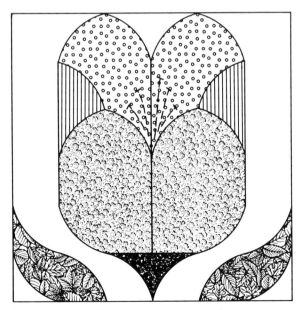

Crocus #1 6 x 6 units

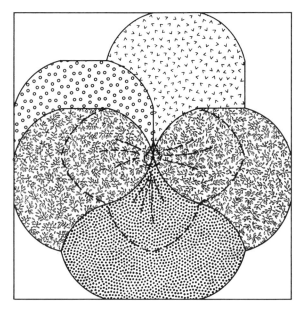

Pansy 6 x 6 units

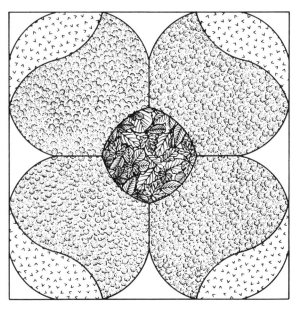

Dogwood 6 x 6 units

Daisy 6 x 6 units

Water Lily 6 x 6 units

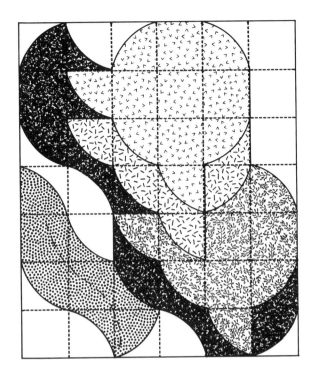

Lily of the Valley 6 x 7 units

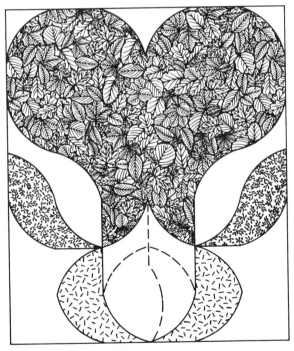
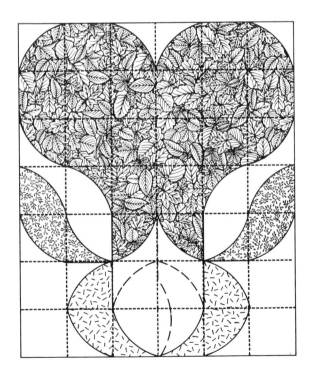

Bleeding Heart 6 x 7 units

49

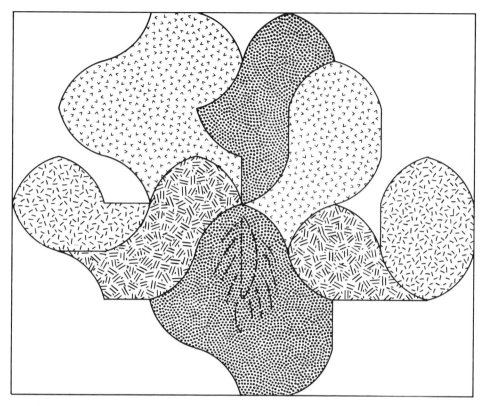

Bearded Iris Medallion 10 x 8 units

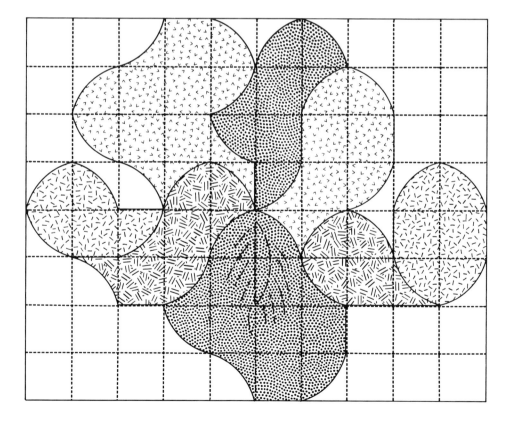

Calla Lilies Medallion 8 x 8 units

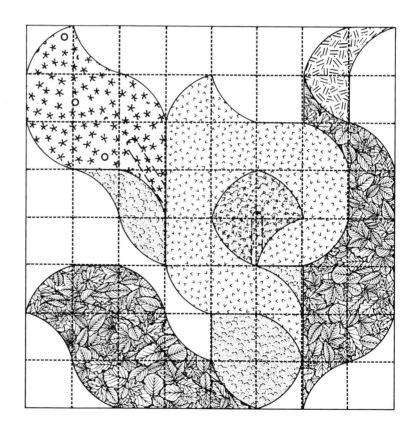

Basket of Blooms Medallion 8 x 8 units

SOME GARDEN COMPANIONS

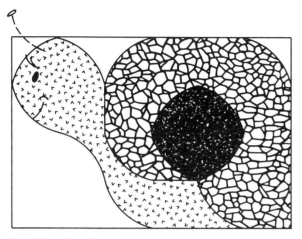

Snail 6 x 4 units

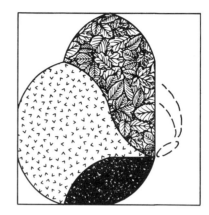

Butterfly 4 x 4 units

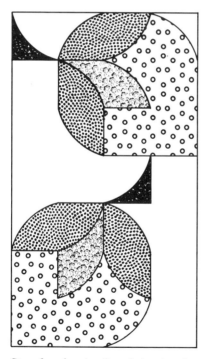
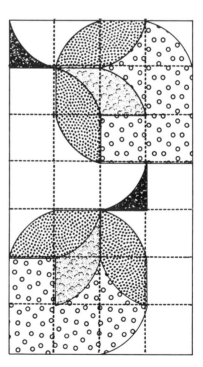

Strawberries 4 x 3 and 4 x 4 units

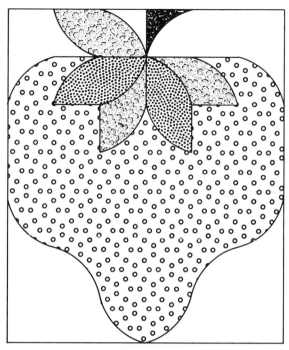

Texas Strawberry 6 x 7 units

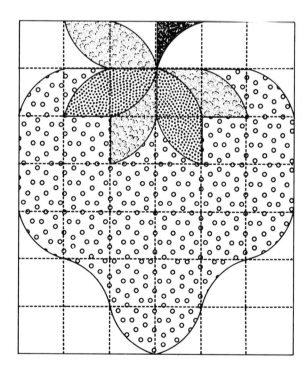

CHAPTER 5

The Borders

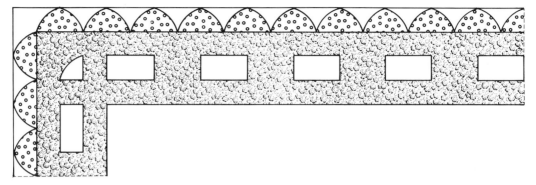

Eyelet Lace

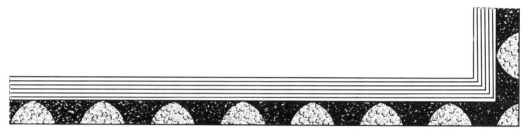

Stamp Edge

Double Scallop

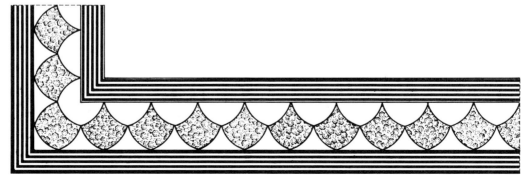

Seashells

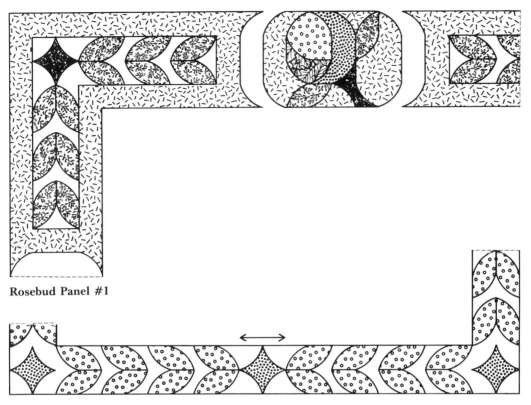

Rosebud Panel #1

Spray of Leaves

Portrait Frame #1

Buds in the Border

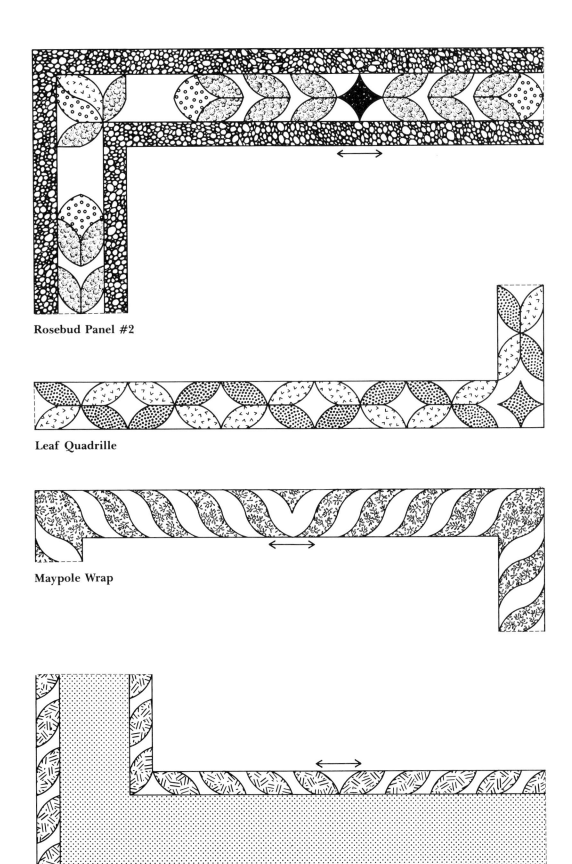

Rosebud Panel #2

Leaf Quadrille

Maypole Wrap

Portrait Frame #2

Victorian Fretwork

Leaves on Parade

Two-toned Leaves

Floret Filigree

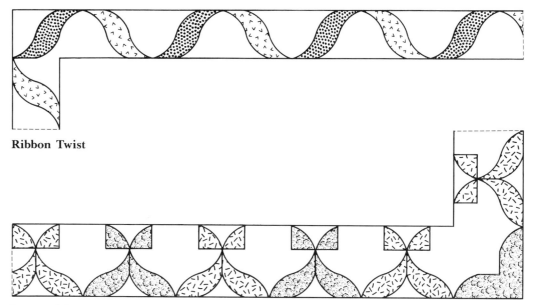

Ribbon Twist

Bow and Swag

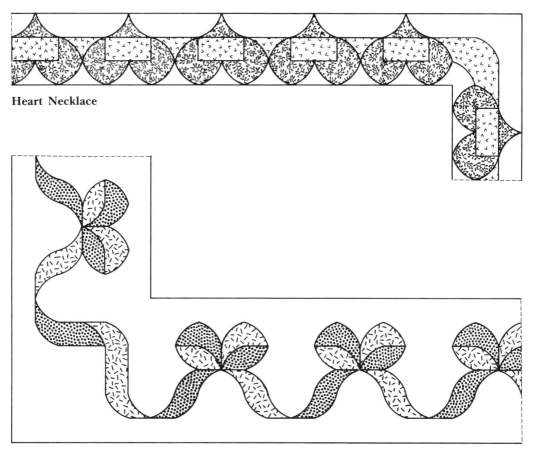

Heart Necklace

Ribbon Bows

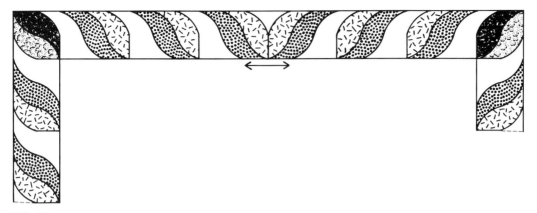

Windblown Leaves

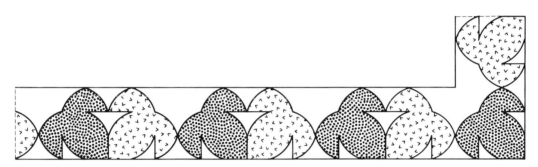

Grape Leaf

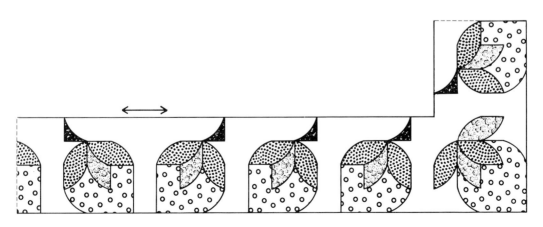

Strawberry Patch (extra spacing row added to center)

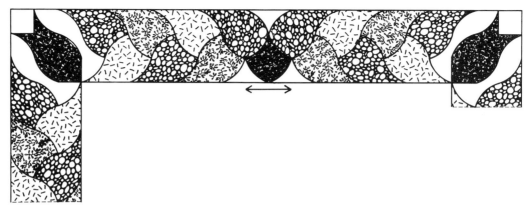

Laurel Braid

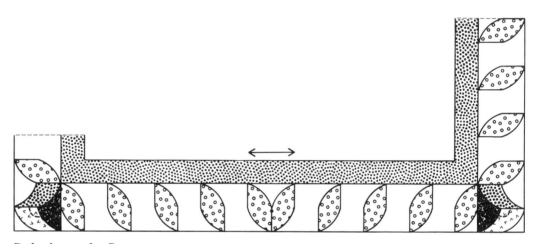

Gathering at the Corner

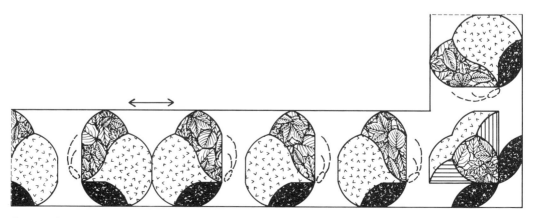

Quest of the Butterfly

The Potted Posy

The Tulip and Its Roots

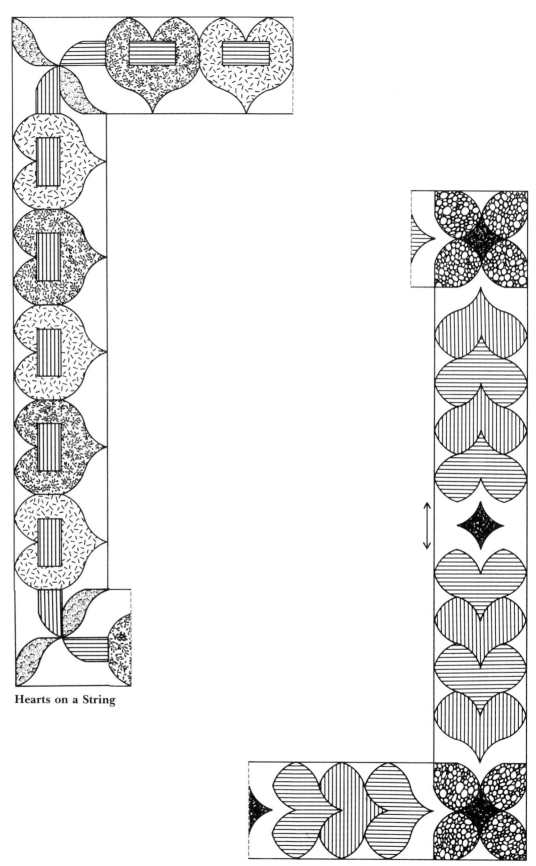

Hearts on a String

Hearts in Concert

Mostly Leaves

Blossoms on the Half Shell

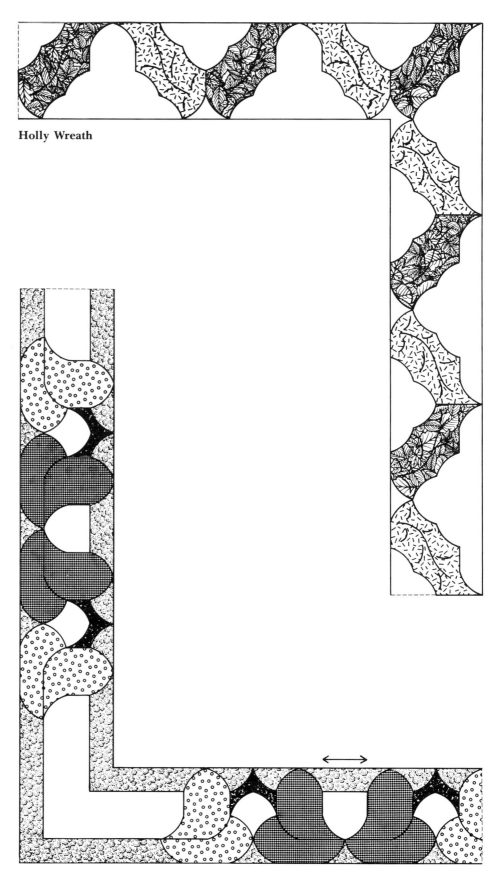

Holly Wreath

Ginger Leaves

Quatrefoil

Bloom Under Glass

68

Lilies of Morocco, 36″ x 56″. Machine-pieced, hand-appliquéd and hand-quilted. By Nancy Vineski, a Joyce Schlotzhauer design.

Album of Pressed Flowers, 45″ x 57″, made by Eulalia Frenzel, designed by Joyce Schlotzhauer. Hand-appliquéd and hand-quilted. The "pressed" flowers are overlaid with organza.

Portland Rose, 56″ x 56″, designed and made by Louise
Hayes. All cottons. Hand-pieced and hand-quilted.

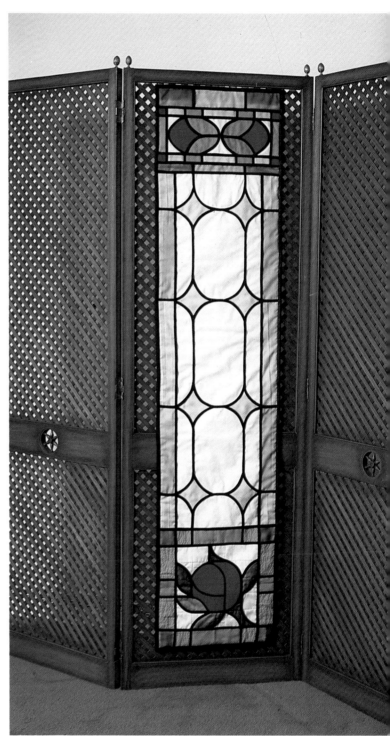

Bell Pull, 8″ x 54″, hand-appliquéd and hand-quilted by Eulalia Frenzel. Design by Joyce Schlotzhauer.

The Stained-glass Rose, 15″ x 63″, by the author. A window quilt, machine-pieced, hand-appliquéd and unquilted.

71

Dutch Bulbs, 84″ x 96″, made by Romayne Bonk and designed by Joyce Schlotzhauer. Cotton fabric innerlined with cotton batiste. Pieced by machine, embroidered and quilted by hand.

CHAPTER 6

The Quilt Designs

Rosebud Wreath

3½″

Rosebud Wreath

Quilt: 77″ x 98″
Template size: 3½″
Rating: Easy

Those who have read the opening chapters already know how to make this quilt. The rosebud was the guinea pig of so many instructional diagrams that it is purposely presented here as a quilt easy enough for beginners. It is shown without patchwork in the border to keep it simple. Like the basic black in fashion, *Rosebud Wreath* can be dressed up or down. If you prefer a more elaborate border, it's a good idea to reduce the template size to 3″. This shrinks the patchwork to fit on top of a double bed. Then you can add 12″ or 15″ borders.

Add seam allowances to all dimensions.

1. Rosebud block: 10½″. Make 48. Refer to chapter 3, "Placement of Templates on Directional Fabric."
2. Join 4 blocks into a square.
3. Repeat step 2 to make 12 squares.
4. Join the squares into rows according to illustration.

Side borders: 7″ x 98″

Top/bottom borders: 7″ x 77″

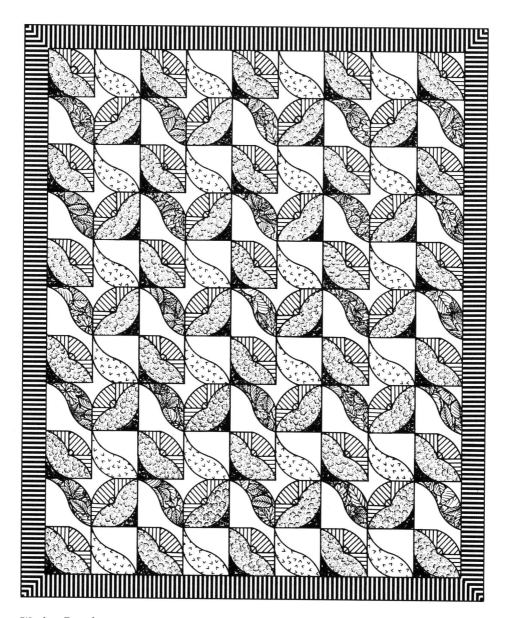

Waving Poppies

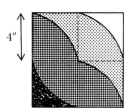

A. Poppy: 8″ x 8″
Make 50.

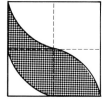

B. Leaf: 8″ x 8″
Make 24.

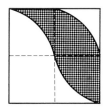

C. Leaf: 8″ x 8″
Make 25.

Waving Poppies
Quilt: 80″ x 96″
Template size: 4″
Rating: Easy

Every time I look at this design, I think of other contemporary versions of the poppy that I've seen. Recently as a house guest, I stayed in a teenager's room that was papered with bold, orange poppies and brown leaves. I've seen blouse fabric with a version striped in black and beige. The banquettes of a restaurant I know are upholstered with enormous peach and white poppies on a sedate background of gray and brown. Maybe I think of contemporary styling because of the flower's simple, cup shape. Maybe it's because I automatically recall the vivid oranges and reds of poppies in nature. At any rate, beginners will find this two-block pattern easy to make and render in many color combinations.

Add seam allowances to all measurements.

Top/bottom borders: 4″ x 80″
Side borders: 4″ x 96″

Order:
1. Assemble in horizontal or vertical rows.
2. Join borders and miter corners.

Pennsylvania Dutch Crib Quilt

Assembly Diagram **Pennsylvania Dutch Crib Quilt**

Pennsylvania Dutch Crib Quilt

Quilt: 45″ x 55″
Template size: 2½″
Rating: Easy

When is a border not a border? When it's bold enough to move to the center as the main attraction. The hearts instantly become the important aspect of the design when they are enlarged to equal the flower. The medallion is a nine-block design that I lengthened into a rectangular quilt by the addition of garlands of leaves. See page 34.

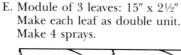

C and C rev. Ribbon tie: 10″ block
Make 2 blocks of each; rotate.
Diagonal corners have identical blocks.

Suggestion: Choose two fabrics for ribbons because one tie lies against portion of ribbon.

Add seam allowances to all measurements.

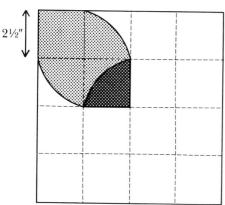

A. Center bluet: 10″ block
Make 4 quarters.
Rotate 90° to form flower.

E. Module of 3 leaves: 15″ x 2½″
Make each leaf as double unit.
Make 4 sprays.

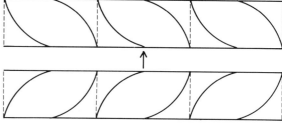

E rev. Module of 3 leaves: 15″ x 2½″
Make 4 sprays.

Note: Background fabric for E, E rev., D and F is the same.

Follow diagram to join and rotate sprays.
D. Make 4: 2½″ x 30″
F. Make 2: 5″ x 50″
G. Make 2: 2½″ x 50″
H. Make 2: 2½″ x 40″
I. Make 4: 2½″ x 2½″

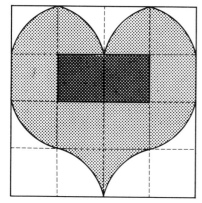

B. Laced heart: 10″ block
Make 4 blocks.
Rotate according to diagram.
Note possible combination patches (see chapter 2).

Order: 1. Assemble medallion in 3 rows of 10″ blocks.

2. Then follow order indicated by letters on diagram.

3. Join the squares I to ends of H.

4. Sew the entire strip (I, H, I) to top and bottom to complete the quilt top.

How to Make and Use a Transparent Overlay of the Assembly Diagram

To calculate dimensions of borders and to see the units of all blocks, you can make a transparent overlay. Place a sheet of tracing paper over the assembly diagram and copy all lines. These indicate the segments, or modules, for assembly. Notice the series of short dashes around the perimeter. With a different colored pencil and a ruler, connect the dashes on the tracing paper with a series of lines across the diagram to form a grid. This will reveal the square units of the quilt and also distinguish them from the assembly modules.

Now place your transparent copy over the quilt illustration. If you have drawn the grid, you see that F is the only border that is two units wide. Count the units of the width and length and multiply each by template size to determine measurements. (Remember to add seam allowances.) The F border is calculated as an example:

$$\begin{array}{cc} 2 \text{ units wide} & \text{by 20 units long} \\ \times\ 2.5'' \text{ template} & \times\ 2.5'' \text{ template} \\ \hline 5'' \text{ wide} & \text{by } 50'' \text{ long (+ seam allowances)} \end{array}$$

Later you may want to use colored pencils on the overlay to experiment with different color combinations.

The copied transparency is also helpful if you want to change the scale of the quilt or convert it to centimeters. It isn't necessary to redraw the blocks. To make the crib quilt smaller, count the number of units across and down (18 × 22 units as shown by the dashes) and multiply by the number of inches or centimeters of a smaller template to determine the width and length.

Examples in inches:

$$\begin{array}{cc} 18 \text{ units across} & \text{by 22 units down} \\ \times\ 2'' \text{ templates} & \times\ 2'' \text{ templates} \\ \hline 36'' \text{ width} & \text{by } 44'' \text{ length} \end{array}$$

Example in centimeters:

$$\begin{array}{cc} 18 \text{ units across} & \text{by 22 units down} \\ \times\ 5 \text{ cm} & \times\ 5 \text{ cm} \\ \hline 90 \text{ cm} & \text{by } 110 \text{ cm} \end{array}$$

The same holds true for enlarging the quilt to double-bed size. The use of 4½" templates will make the quilt 81" × 99". (Enlargement of this particular quilt is not a recommendation, merely an exercise. The resulting 18" blocks of hearts would not have the charm of the smaller ones.) The same method for enlarging or reducing applies to the other quilts that are presented with assembly diagrams. Rescale quilts of repeated blocks by changing the template size for the block (see chapter 3, "Template Size Determines Block Measurement"). Then multiply the new block size by the number of times you will repeat it, both across and down.

Glorified Vine

Glorified Vine

Quilt: 84″ x 98″
Template size: 3½″
Rating: Easy

This four-block repeat assembles quickly. One block has only a few patches, and two blocks have large, uncut rectangles. There's plenty of open space for special quilting. Why not think of the vine climbing a wall and do straight-lined quilting in a brick pattern?

As a design exercise, remove from block A and D the tip of the longest leaf (an A patch). If you cut these two patches from the background fabric for each set of blocks, two-unit wide columns appear between the vines. Then with a smaller template and an extra color, you can achieve a totally different pattern.

Add seam allowances to all measurements.

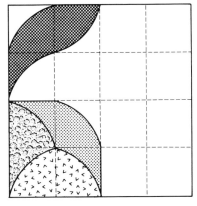

Block B: 14″ x 14″
Make 11.

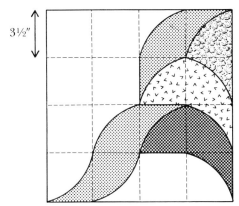

3½″

Block A: 14″ x 14″
Make 11.

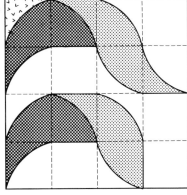

Block D: 14″ x 14″
Make 9.
Make the 10th one according to instruction 4.

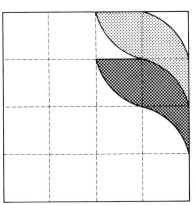

Block C: 14″ x 14″
Make 10.

Order: 1. Join blocks A, B, C, D into squares of 4 to make 9 large blocks according to the illustration.
2. Sew 3 large squares (A, B, C, D) into vertical vines. Repeat to make 3.
3. To the bottom of first and third vine, sew an A and B block that have been joined.
4. To the top of the middle vine, sew a C and D block that have been joined.
Note: *Replace the base of the flower with background fabric in this D block.
5. Join the 3 vines vertically.

Cornered Daisy

84

Cornered Daisy

Quilt: 80″ x 95″
Template size: 2½″
Rating: Easy

Why not have the focal point of your quilt in a corner arrangement? Ever notice how elegantly wrapped packages have the bow off-center? This is the same idea. There are 15″ to the left and bottom that allow for ample drop and a rim of background on the edge of the bed. In this way the design flows over the edge without appearing in danger of completely slipping off. Of course such a pattern must be counter-balanced with lots of quilting. Choose this design because you enjoy hand-quilting, not because of the small amount of patchwork.

Add seam allowances to all measurements.

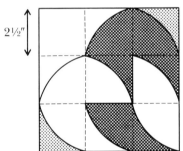

A. Painted Daisy (¼) 7½″ x 7½″
Make 4.
Rotate and join to complete flower.
Note: Leaf tips included.

B. Appliqués: 5″ sides
Make 4.
Appliqué to corners of panels.

C. Leaf: 5″ x 5″
Make 29.

C rev.: 5″ x 5″
Make 29.

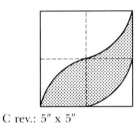

D. Join rows of C and C rev.
Upper vertical: 13 blocks of each.
Right side: 10 blocks of each.
Left side: 3 blocks of each.
Bottom: 3 blocks of each.

Spacing bands for either side of leaf rows:
E. Upper vertical: 2½″ x 65″ Make 2.
F. Right horizontal: 2½″ x 50″ Make 2.
G. Left horizontal and lower vertical: 2½″ x 15″ Make 4.

Panels: I. Upper right: 50″ x 65″
        J. Lower right: 50″ x 15″
        K. Upper left: 15″ x 65″
        L. Lower left: 15″ x 15″

Order: 1. Join a spacing band to each side of leaf rows.
        2. Join K, completed leaf rows with bands and I.
        3. Join horizontal leaf rows with bands to either side of flower.
        4. Join L, completed leaf rows with bands and J.
        5. Complete by joining the 3 sections horizontally.

Waltz of the Flowers

Waltz of the Flowers

Quilt: 36″ x 57″
Template sizes: 1″ (for appliqué patterns), 2″ and 3″
Rating: Intermediate

The interrelationship of patchwork blocks is fascinating to all of us. This pattern for a wall hanging could mesmerize the uninitiated viewer. One pattern does it all, but to keep repetition from becoming too tiresome, I used three scales and also inverted one row. Only the intervening horizontal bands control the curves. And if the flowers aren't waltzing, they have their petals linked on high in some grand promenade. Refer to a rendition on page 69 to see the effect of color and print fabrics.

Add seam allowances to all measurements.

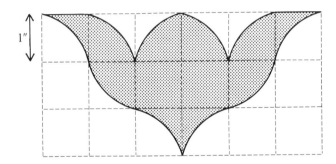

Flower for appliqué: 3″ x 6″

1. Trace and cut 1″ patchwork templates. See template sheet at end of chapter 3.
2. To make appliqué template:
   a. Draw 1″ squares on graph paper.
   b. Use 1″ patchwork templates to outline flower.
   c. Transfer outline to template material and cut.
3. Cut 22 whole flowers and 4 halves (2 of each side).
4. Cut 2 background strips: 4″ x 36″.

Dimensions of strips between rows numbered from the top:
1″ x 36″: strips 2, 3
2″ x 36″: strips 1, 4, 5, 6
3″ x 36″: strip 7
(Widths are optional)

To complete the 2 appliqué strips:
1. Center one flower in length of strip (4″ x 36″).
2. Lay out appliqués according to illustration and check spacing. Appliqué starting from center.

Assemble in horizontal rows.

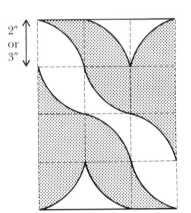

Patchwork flower block:

1. For 3 rows, use 2″ templates: 6″ x 8″ block. Make 3 blocks and 3 reverse blocks for each row. (Third row is rotated 180°)
2. For fourth row, use 3″ templates: 9″ x 12″ block. Make 2 blocks and 2 rev. blocks.

. . . How Does Your Garden Grow?

Quilt: 78″ x 96″
Template size: 3″
Rating: Intermediate

Like this design, my grandmother's flower garden had a delightful mix of flowers. She planted her flowers as she did the vegetable patch, in neat rows. This idea, translated into a kind of sampler of the Curved Two-Patch flowers, gave me the opportunity to use the *Pansy*, a favorite of those who have seen the flower designs. It's a large flower (at least it is in my quilt garden), so I used only four across the foot of the bed. My mother, who was a horticultural judge, would have said, "You ought to plant the tallest flowers to the back." But I'm the quilter. I use that as an excuse whenever it's necessary. Also see page 124.

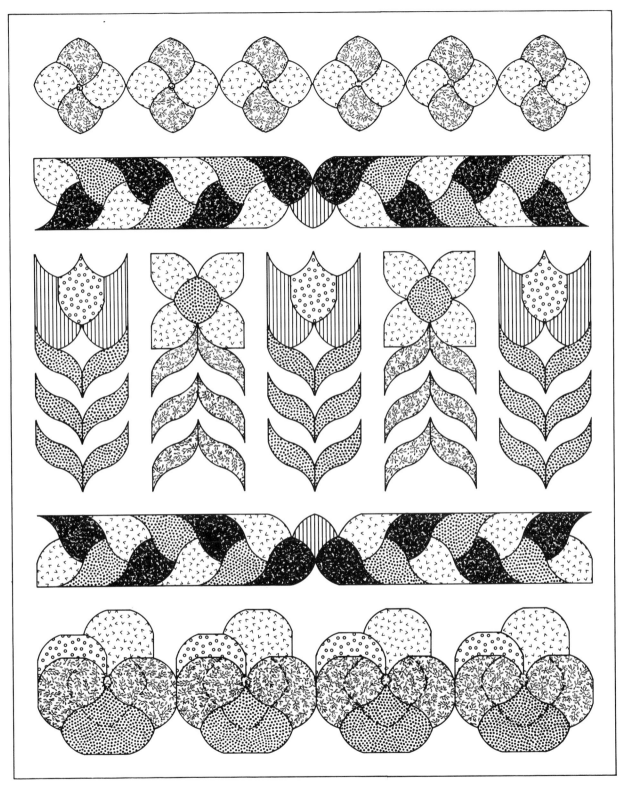

. . . How Does Your Garden Grow?

. . . How Does Your Garden Grow?

Add seam allowances to all measurements.

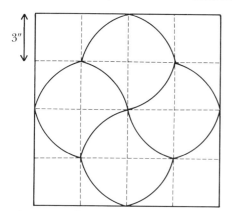

3"

A. Posy: 12" x 12"
   Make 6.

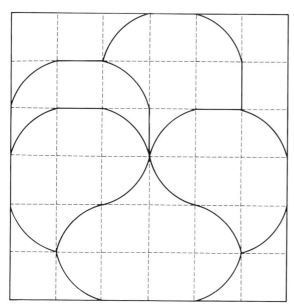

B. Pansy: 18" x 18"
   Make 4.

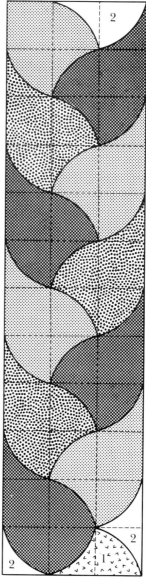

C. Half braid: 9" x 36"
   Make 2 and 2 rev.

In the braid:

1. Half bud.
2. Background fabric.

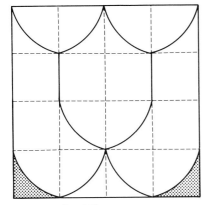

D. Tulip: 12″ x 12″
   Make 3.

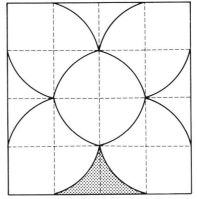

E. Bluet: 12″ x 12″
   Make 2.

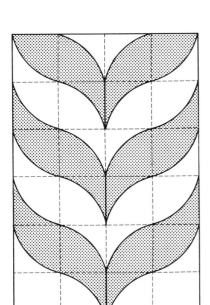

F. Leaves for tulip: 12″ x 18″
   Make 3.

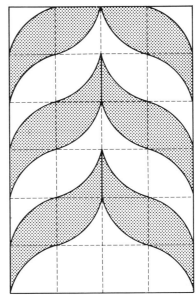

G. Leaves for bluet: 12″ x 18″
   Make 2.

H. Vertical spacing bands between flowers with leaves: 3″ x 30″
   Make 4.

I. Horizontal spacing bands between rows: 3″ x 72″
   Make 4.

J. Top/bottom borders: 3″ x 78″

K. Side borders: 3″ x 96″

Order: Assemble in horizontal rows. Add borders and miter corners.

Rose After Rose

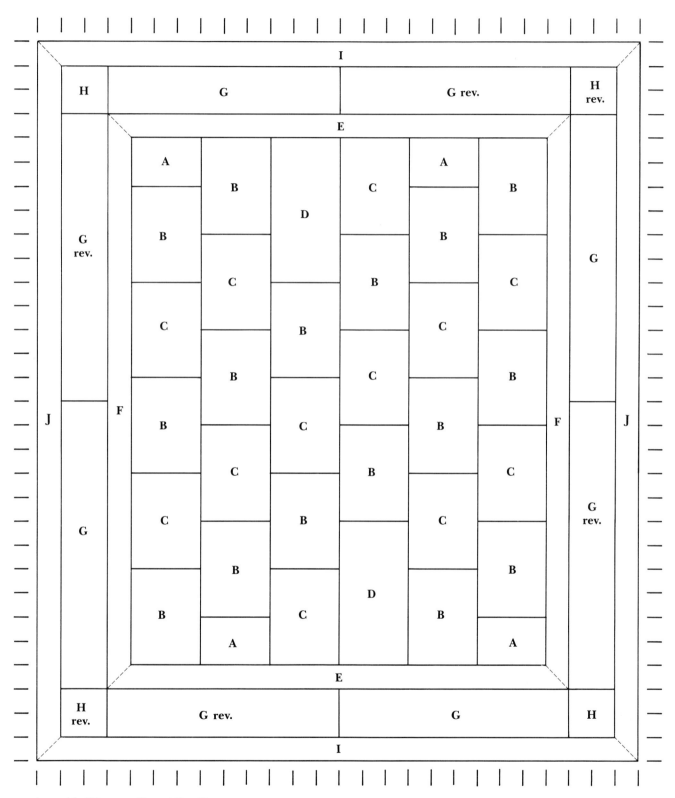

Assembly Diagram **Rose After Rose**

Rose After Rose

Quilt: 78″ x 90″
Template size: 3″
Rating: Intermediate

When it was time to name this quilt, I thought of the "Parade of Roses," the New Year's Day classic. While football fans are only starting to gather around the television for the coming game, I am staring in awe at all those thousands and thousands of roses so meticulously arranged on fanciful floats. Like marchers in full-dress uniforms, the blossoms appear in parade formations. In this design, a chorus line of rosebuds marches diagonally up and down the quilt top in a drop, repeat arrangement. I had to cheat a bit to prevent cutting two of the asymmetrical rosebud blocks in half. (The two outside diagonal rows would have half buds, if I had continued the arrangement.) I decided to treat the half blocks as background, so you will find them added to the rectangles (D).

Refer to page 81 for directions if you want to make a transparent overlay of the assembly diagram.

Add seam allowances to all measurements.

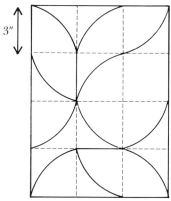

3″

B. Rosebud: 9″ x 12″ block
Make 16.
Rotate following diagram.

A. 9″ x 6″: Make 4.
C. 9″ x 12″: Make 12.
D. 9″ x 18″: Make 2.
E. 3″ x 60″: Make 2.
F. 3″ x 72″: Make 2.
I. 3″ x 78″: Make 2.
J. 3″ x 90″: Make 2.

Order: 1. Assemble the patchwork blocks of the body of the quilt in vertical rows.

2. Add borders E and F. Note: Measurements reflect mitered corners.

3. Join sets of leaves as instructed. Note: The groups on sides of quilt require an extra set (6 sets vs. 5 sets for the top and bottom).

4. Join G and G rev. to top and bottom.

5. Add H and H rev. to G and G rev. for sides and join to quilt.

6. Add borders I and J and miter corners.

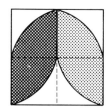

G. Leaf module: 6″ x 6″
Make each leaf as double unit: 3″ x 6″.
Note: Leaves are mirror images.
Make 22 of each leaf.
Join to form sets of 2 leaves as shown.
Follow diagram for placement (G).

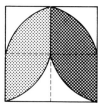

G rev. Repeat instructions for G, but join to form sets of 2 leaves as shown here.

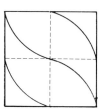

H and H rev. corner bud: 6″ block
Make 2 of each; rotate.

The Occasional Orchid

The Occasional Orchid

Quilt: 75¾″ x 93⅜″
Template size: 2½″
Rating: Intermediate

Orchids seem to combine better with ribbons than with leaves. This design displays the "prom-night special" with twisted, looped and tied ribbons in a diagonal assembly. The width of the border and ribbons is the same, but you can increase the border width to enlarge the quilt's dimensions. The cascading ribbons give so much movement to the quilt that a complicated border is unnecessary.

I know we don't usually think of occasional orchids by the dozen. It just turned out that way.

Add seam allowances to all measurements.

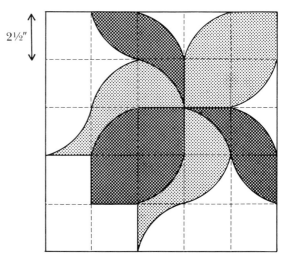

2½″

A. Orchid block: 12½″ x 12½″
Make 12.

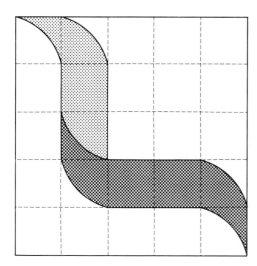

B. Ribbon block: 12½″ x 12½″
Make 8.
Rows 2, 4

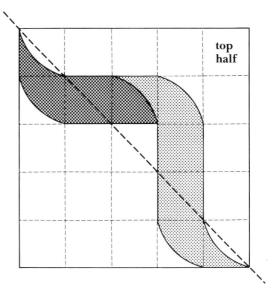

top half

C. Ribbon block: 12½″ x 12½″
Make 12 for rows 1, 3, 5.
Make 8 top halves for side blocks.
Or piece the 6 patches and appliqué to ½ block of background.

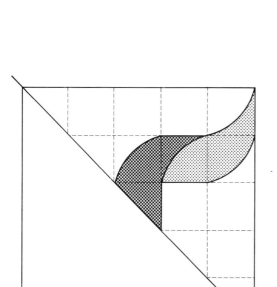

D. Top/bottom half blocks.
Make 6.
The 6 patches can be pieced and then appliquéd to a half block of background.

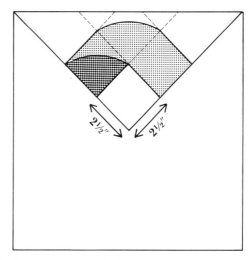

2½″   2½″

E. Corner quarter blocks.
Make 4.

Piece the 4 patches, then appliqué to ¼ block of background.

For appliqué blocks, each color of ribbon can be cut as one appliqué and sewn to the partial blocks.

Top/bottom borders: 2½″ x 75¾″

Side borders: 2½″ x 93⅜″

Order:
Assemble in diagonal rows. Remember, the ribbons alternate when the design is viewed diagonally.

Leafy Bower

Quilt: 80″ x 100″
Template size: 2½″
Rating: Intermediate or advanced (depending on fabric choice)

After the fun of designing a quilt, the time always comes for mundane decisions of construction methods. Although there are several approaches that would work, I thought you might like the advantages of this lattice-strip assembly. (1) The large, blank squares are available for adding flowers. (2) If the squares are left whole, there will be no seam allowances to interfere with intricate quilting patterns. (3) Rather than patch the side strips to complete the leaves that jut out from the design, cut the strips full length and appliqué the patches.

This pattern is tricky. In case you haven't noticed as yet, the two sets of leaves are mirror images. It's easier to make the quilt with one nondirectional print for all leaves. Even so, half of these in each lattice strip will be reverses. With two leaf fabrics, you will have reverse leaves to cut from each. If this is your preference, don't do anything without checking the illustration first! The design is organized with the extra interest of a second leaf fabric, but you must be alert when matching strips and appliqués to the lattice corners.

Leafy Bower

Diagram showing lower left corner of quilt.

Leafy Bower

Add seam allowances to all measurements.

A. Lattice corner: 5″ x 5″
   Make 10.

B. Vertical double row of leaves: 5″ x 15″ (single leaf in a double unit: 2½″ x 5″)
   Make 16.

C. Alternate lattice corner: 5″ x 5″
   Make 10.

D. Blank square: 15″ x 15″
   Make 12.

E. Crosswise double row of leaves: 5″ x 15″
   Make 15.

F. Side strips with appliquéd patches: 2½″ x 85″
   Make 2.

G. Top/bottom strips with appliqué patches: 2½″ x 70″
   Make 2.

H. Side borders: 5″ x 90″
   Make 2.

I. Top/bottom borders: 5″ x 80″
   Make 2.

J. Appliqués to complete leaves for side strips (F)
   Make 10.

K. Appliqués to complete alternate leaves for top/bottom strips (G)
   Make 8.

Order:

1. Assemble vertical lattice strips by alternating the corners (A and C) and rotating the rows of leaves (B) 180° according to the illustration.

2. Join crosswise lattice strips (E) to blank squares (D) to form vertical columns.
   Rotate the strips 180° following illustration.

3. Join the assembled vertical lattice to combinations of D and E.

4. Line up side strip (F) with body of the quilt and carefully mark placement of the 5 (J) appliqué patches adjacent to the incomplete leaves of lattice corners.
   Appliqué and join strip to quilt.

5. Repeat step 4 to join other F strip to opposite side.

6. Repeat step 4 for top/bottom strips (G). There are 4 (K) appliqués per strip.

7. Join borders (H) to the sides and (I) to top and bottom to complete the quilt top.

Woodland Favorites

Quilt: 84″ x 96″
Template size: 3″
Rating: Advanced

Many of the lovely antique quilts were made of only four blocks and an elaborate swag border. The ones that come to mind, however, were appliquéd. This quilt is a patchwork adaptation of that concept. The flowers aren't really difficult, but they require some patience because the design isn't revealed until several rows of patched units are joined.

The border design breaks one of my rules: Corners are always treated as corners. In the diagrams you can see that there is no corner square in the twisted ribbon. The top and bottom borders overlap the sides to complete the twist of the ribbons.

Woodland Favorites

Woodland Favorites

Add seam allowances to all measurements.

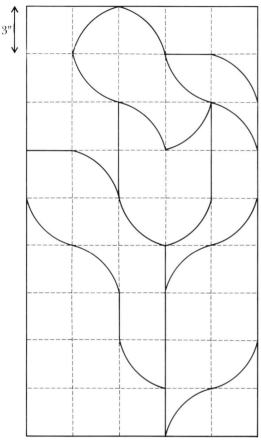

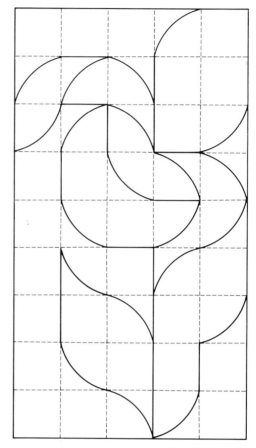

A. Block (with spacing rows): 21″ x 27″
   Jack-in-the-Pulpit: 15″ x 27″

1. Make 1 and 1 reverse.

2. Assemble in horizontal rows.

3. For A reverse, copy diagram with tracing paper and flip over.

4. Cut 2 spacing rows (C): 3″ x 27″.
   Join to sides to complete the block.

B. Block (with spacing rows): 21″ x 27″
   Lady Slipper: 15″ x 27″

1. Make 1 and 1 reverse.

2. Assemble in horizontal rows.

3. For B reverse, copy diagram with tracing paper and flip over.

4. Cut 2 spacing rows (C): 3″ x 27″.
   Join to sides to complete the block.

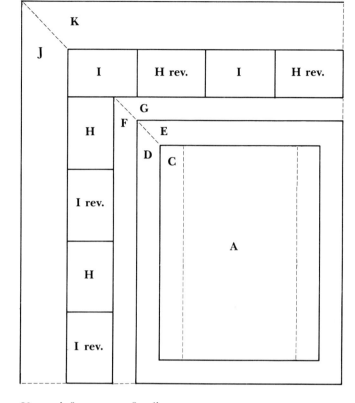

Upper left quarter of quilt.

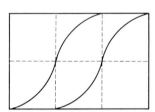

H and I Ribbon Twist: 9″ x 6″

H fabric #1: Make 8 and 8 reverse.

I fabric #2: Make 8 and 8 reverse.

C. Spacing rows in all flower blocks: 3″ x 27″
   Make 8.

D. Side frames for each flower block: 3″ x 33″
   Make 8.

E. Top/bottom frames for each flower block: 3″ x 27″
   Make 8.

F. Side frames for the 4 blocks: 3″ x 72″
   Make 2.

G. Top/bottom frames for the 4 blocks: 3″ x 60″
   Make 2.

J. Side borders: 6″ x 96″
   Make 2.

K. Top/bottom borders: 6″ x 84″
   Make 2.

Order:

1. Complete each flower by adding spacing rows (C) and frame (D, E).

2. Join the 4 framed flower blocks.

3. Sew frame (F, G) to the 4 blocks.

4. Alternately join 8 blocks of H and I reverse (follow diagram and illustration). Sew to one side of quilt. Repeat for the opposite side.

5. Following diagram, alternately join 8 blocks of I and H reverse. Sew to the top of quilt. Repeat for the bottom of quilt.

6. Sew on borders (J and K) and miter the corners.

Dutch Bulbs

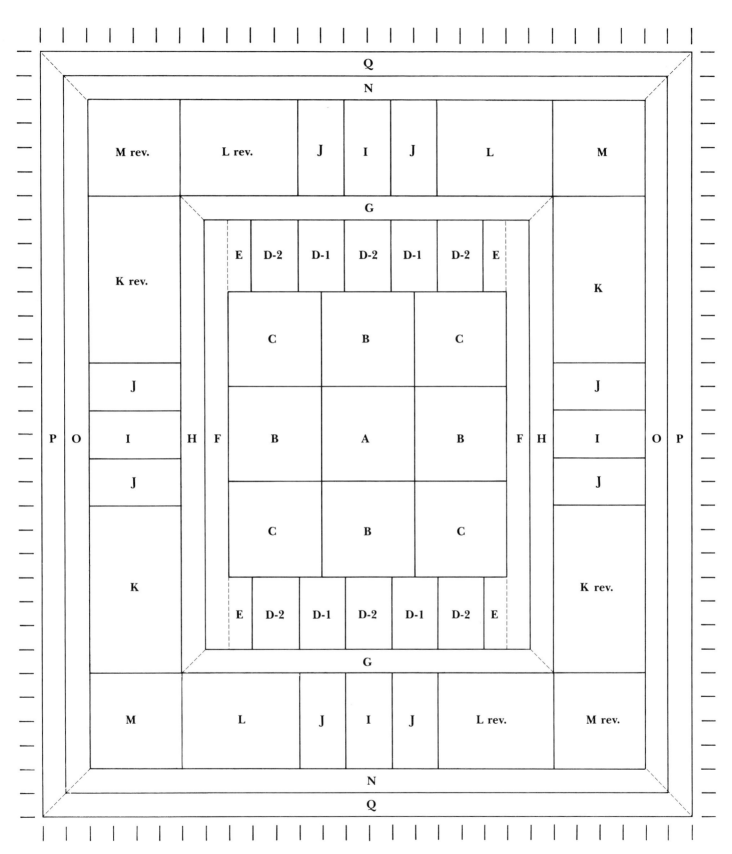

Assembly Diagram **Dutch Bulbs**

Dutch Bulbs

Quilt: 84″ x 96″
Template size: 3″
Rating: Advanced

Maybe intermarriage between the Pennsylvania German sects is not common, but I've arranged a match with this pattern. The stylized tulips perched above long, leafy stems certainly have a Pennsylvania Dutch flavor. To elongate the center square into a rectangle, I borrowed the Amish use of bars. Layered on top is a medallion of more tulips. This is to suggest a hex sign nailed to a barn of board and batten. For the quilt on page 72, I selected Amish colors to enhance the blending of the two styles. It would look more Pennsylvania Dutch with strong reds, yellows and greens. Romayne Bonk, who made the quilt, thought of doing it in the delft blue and white of Dutch tiles. That too would be a pleasing color choice.

Add seam allowances to all measurements.

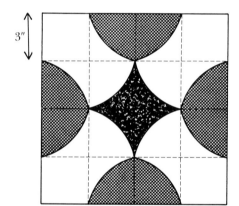

A. Center block: 12″ x 12″
   Make 1.

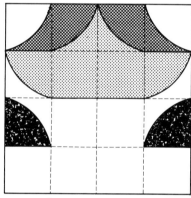

B. Partial tulip: 12″ x 12″
   Make 4.

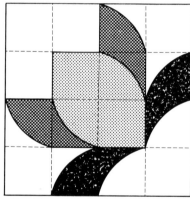

C. Corner block of medallion: 12″ x 12″
   Make 4.

108

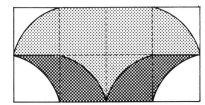

J. Border module: 12″ x 6″
   Make 8.

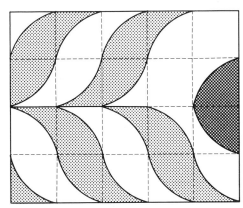

L. Top/bottom border module: 12″ x 15″
   Make 2.

L rev. Make 2.

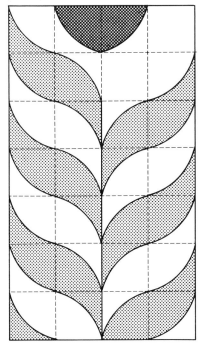

K. Side border module: 12″ x 21″
   Make 2.

K rev. Copy diagram on tracing paper and flip over.
   Make 2.

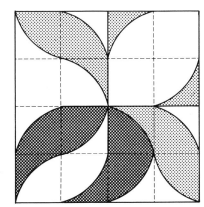

M. Corner of border: 12″ x 12″
   Make 2.

M rev. Make 2.

D-1. Fabric #1: 6″ x 9″ module   Make 4.
D-2. Fabric #2: 6″ x 9″ module   Make 6.
   E. Fabric same as D-1: 3″ x 9″ module   Make 4.
   F. Fabric same as D-1: 3″ x 54″ strip   Make 2.
   G. Strip: 3″ x 48″   Make 2.
   H. Strip: 3″ x 60″   Make 2.
   I. Module: 12″ x 6″   Make 4.
   N. Strip: 3″ x 78″   Make 2.
   O. Strip: 3″ x 90″   Make 2.
   P. Strip: 3″ x 96″   Make 2.
   Q. Strip: 3″ x 84″   Make 2.

Order: 1. Assemble medallion in 3 rows.
   2. Join bars (D-1, D-2, E) together according to diagram
      and join to top/bottom.
   3. Sew strips (F) to sides.
   4. Sew strips (G) to top/bottom.
   5. Sew strips (H) to sides.
   6. Follow diagram to sew I, J, K, K rev., and sew to sides.
   7. Follow diagram to sew I, J, L, L rev., M, M rev., and
      sew to top/bottom.
   8. Sew strips (N, O) to quilt top.
   9. Complete by sewing strips (P, Q) to quilt top.

Garden Borders

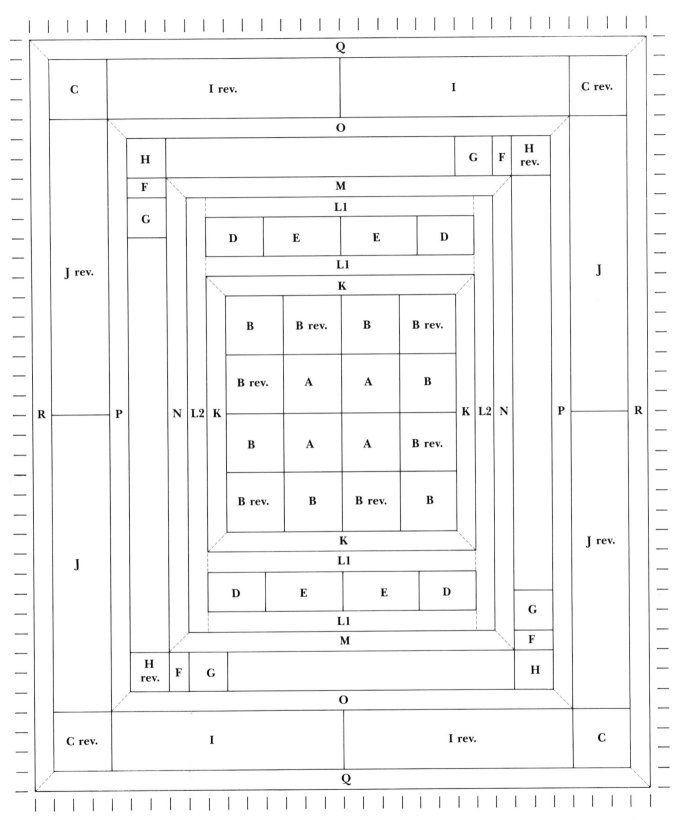

Assembly Diagram **Garden Borders**

Garden Borders

Quilt: 80" x 95"
Template size: 2½"
Rating: Advanced

Although there are two or three quilts in this group that have medallions, this is the only one that is ringed with a number of varied borders. The medallion style of quilt, currently so popular, is a natural choice for the flowers of the Curved Two-Patch System. This design reminds me of the grand estates of the past that had formal gardens with manicured paths between the showy plants and shrubs. You join the ranks of the landed gentry when you choose to make *Garden Borders*.

The fact that there are borders of repeated blocks helps you break the work down to a manageable size. The outer braided leaf border, admittedly, has to be patched, unit by unit, and demands close attention to the diagram. But once it's done, it's done. No need to weed and feed! Also see page 35.

Add seam allowances to all measurements.

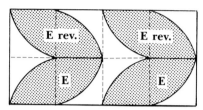

E. Leaf sprays: 10" x 5"
Make 4.

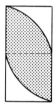

F. Leaf for bell blossom: 2½" x 5"
Make 28.

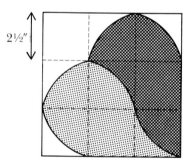

A. Center flower (¼): 7½" x 7½"
Make 4.
Rotate and join.
Completed flower: 15" x 15"

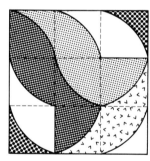

C. Bluebonnet in outer border: 7½" x 7½"
Make 2.
Make 2 reverse.

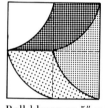

G. Bell blossom: 5" x 5"
Make 28.

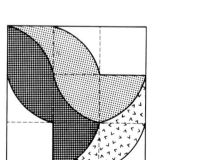

B. Bluebonnet in medallion: 7½" x 7½"
Make 6.
Make 6 reverse.

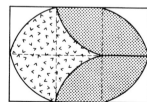

D. Bud: 7½" x 5"
Make 4.
Background fabric is same as L-1, L-2.

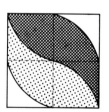

H. Corner bud: 5" x 5"
Make 2 and 2 rev.

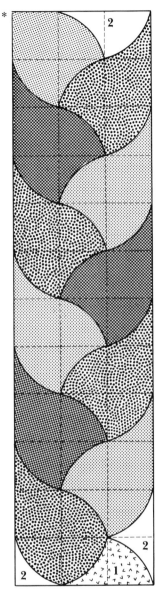

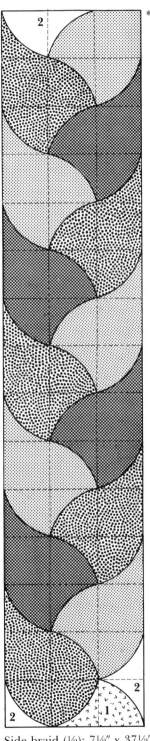

I. Top/bottom braid (½): 7½" x 30"
Make 2 and 2 rev.

Notes for I and J:
*Tip of this leaf is in block C.
1. One-half of center bud.
2. Background fabric.

J. Side braid (½): 7½" x 37½"
Make 2 and 2 rev.

K. Border for medallion: 2½" x 35"   Make 4.

L-1. Spacing bands: 2½" x 35"   Make 4.

L-2. Same fabric as L-1: 2½" x 55"   Make 2.

M. Inner borders for bell blossom: 2½" x 45"
Make 2.

N. Inner borders for bell blossom: 2½" x 60"
Make 2.

O. Inner borders for braids: 2½" x 60"   Make 2.

P. Inner borders for braids: 2½" x 75"   Make 2.

Q. Outer borders: 2½" x 80"   Make 2.

R. Outer borders: 2½" x 95"   Make 2.

About the order of assembly:

Closely follow both assembly diagram and quilt illustration for joining blocks and borders, starting in the center and working outward. Copying the diagram on tracing paper and overlaying it on the illustration is a small chore that is worth the effort.

You may wonder why block C in the assembly diagram has a letter that seems out of order. I chose to illustrate this bluebonnet next to block B to point out its difference.

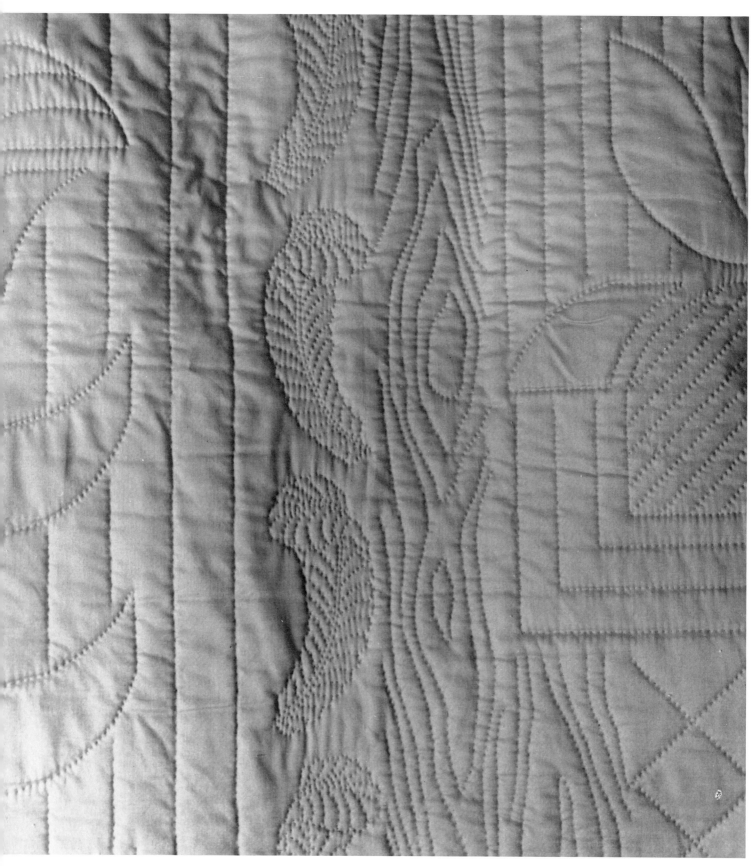

Detail of **Dutch Bulbs** showing the quilting on the reverse side. The feather and wood-grain quilting, designed by the author, occur in the black bands and the deep blue bars, respectively.

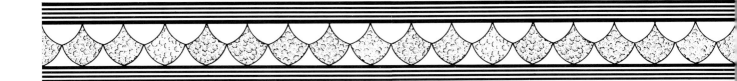

CHAPTER 7

Working With the Designs

Generally, we patchworkers think of a quilt block as a square. We assume it will be repeated and developed into an abstract design and often expect a secondary design to emerge with the arrangement of the blocks. Some of the patterns of this book fit those assumptions. Others do not. Because a quilt block by any other name is still a quilt block, I use that term. But be aware of differences. Some blocks are rectangles. Many are asymmetrical designs and are not good choices as repeat patterns without separation. These designs of curved patches are more pictorial than abstract and, therefore, call for special handling.

The flower blocks could be categorized by flower genus or by size. The first category is useful to horticulturists, not patchworkers. For the second, I have grouped the floral designs by their number of units in a list on page 131. But for design purposes, let's investigate the shapes of the blocks and how the flowers are presented within them. The blocks are mainly squares plus a few wide and long rectangles. We need to break down the largest category of squares because the flowers appear in three distinct ways.

◇ Squares With Flowers in Three Positions

The symmetrical flower patterns are the ones most similar to traditional patchwork. They have one important advantage: They are the only designs that can logically be divided and used as half or quarter blocks when you need the quilt a little wider or longer, or when partial blocks help you center a design. Louise Hayes used this design method for her *Portland Rose*. She pieced quarter blocks as repeated suggestions of the center starflower. (See page 70.)

The flowers of this category can be repeated without any separation, but the "tiling" effect of the four corners will be noticeably different from that of other geometric blocks. Look at figure 25a. Because a con-

siderable portion of each of the dogwood petals reaches the edges of the block, the floral quality is somewhat diminished and the secondary pattern becomes prominent. Figure 25b shows another secondary design. But because the petals of the starflower barely touch each other, the flowers still dominate the design.

Some flowers set diagonally in squares also have attractive tiling patterns when repeated. (See *Rosebud Wreath* in chapter 6.) In *Garden Borders* (same chapter) the bluebonnets touch each other around the rim of the floral medallion. With the relief of pattern in the center, all flowers are recognizable. In *Dried Arrangement* by Shirley Harkness and Marjory Harris, page 35, notice how color also helps to separate design elements. In the quilts, the abstract quality of the bluebonnets enhances the medallion. However, on replacing the center medallion with four more bluebonnets (fig. 26), an ornate cross appears, and the flowers are lost. The curves undulate across the repeats. That is not necessarily undesirable, unless you really wanted bluebonnets.

The easiest way to see if you like the repeat of a pattern is to place a sheet of tracing paper over the flower block. Trace it, rotate the tracing paper 90° and trace it again. Repeat the rotation of the tracing paper two more times to form a square of four blocks (fig. 27a). This process should be continued until you have 16 blocks. (In figure 26, if I had stopped with four blocks, we would not see the cross pattern.) Did the pattern suffer from too much rotation? It may be better to draw two blocks as mirror images. Start the same exercise again, but this time flip the tracing paper over and copy two blocks in diagonal corners (fig. 27b). The paper is transparent enough for you to see the reversed blocks once the paper is turned again to the right side. Of course, if you eventually decide upon this grouping, you will want to draw it on graph

Fig. 25. Tiling effects of symmetrical flowers.

a. Four blocks of the *Dogwood Blossom.*

Fig. 26. Mosaic effect of sixteen *Bluebonnet* blocks.

b. Four blocks of the *Starflower.*

paper and mark the mirror images as reversals. Many of you may be adept at visualizing secondary patterns of geometric blocks, but because of these curves, I feel it is important to try the repetitions on paper.

If you tried tracing multiples of a design and ended with a disaster, chances are that you have chosen an asymmetrical flower. The tiger lily and the iris are two examples that do not like the proximity of three more of their kind (fig. 28). For these I have added companion blocks to help separate them in a quilt. (See chapter 4.) The tiger lily has its own drooping bud surrounded by leaves. The iris can be combined with its upright, "wrapped" bud. These two companion designs do not fill the blocks; they have vertical rows on each side that are blank units. Call them spacing rows. These will be cut as strips and sewn to the patchwork units. Now try tracing combinations of the buds and their parent flowers.

◇ **Flowers in Long and Wide Rectangles**

There are only a few flowers in this category. Originally, there were a great many, but working with them over a period of time, I converted most into squares. As a suggested design for long rectangles, the lady slipper and jack-in-the-pulpit are matched up in the quilt, *Woodland Favorites,* (chapter 6). The length of these flower blocks also makes them good choices for wall art. A single patchwork flower of a large scale can be framed as a botanical print. Long rectangles also have a distinct advantage as center medallions. Because they are already elongated, there is no need to

Fig. 27. Four repeats of asymmetrical flower block.

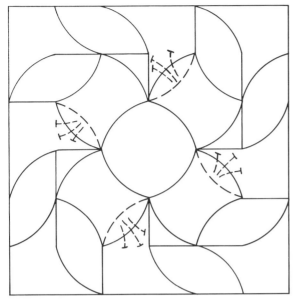

a. *Trumpet Vine* repeated by rotation of blocks.

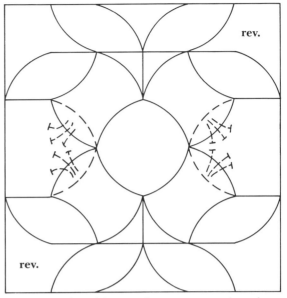

b. *Trumpet Vine* with opposite corners as mirror images or reversals.

contrive some trick to change a quilt design from a square to a long rectangle. Some of the buds are also long rectangles. These small, narrow blocks can substitute as lattice strips. Thus, you can design a variation of *Leafy Bower*, one of the illustrated quilts in chapter 6. Your choice of buds can replace the sprays of leaves.

A rectangular block that is wider than long is more challenging to work with when you need to determine the dimensions of a quilt. Two methods for lengthening a wide block are shown among the photographed examples. Linda Halpin wanted to make a version of . . . *How Does Your Garden Grow?* to use as a panel for a glass door (page 124). I drew the *Bearded Iris*, a wide rectangle, as a heading and then added panels of floral repeats to lengthen it. Of course a single block of the *Bearded Iris* could be made as a wall hanging for those places that need something wide. To use as a center medallion, try adding garlands of leaves above and below or groups of butterflies to lengthen the iris. *Stylized Lily #2* and *Waltzing Tulips*, also wide rectangles, have profile shapes that lend themselves to a contemporary treatment. I like them in horizontal bands. In *Waltz of the Flowers* (chapter 6), I diminished the importance of the flowers by allowing their edges to touch and the curves to wave continuously across the quilt. Horizontal bands of fabric separate the rows and add length to the quilt. For *Lilies of Morocco*, I asked Nancy Vineski to interpret the design using border prints for the lengthening bands. Refer to page 69 for the effect of color and

Fig. 28. Avoid the awkward tiling effect of some asymmetrical flower blocks.

pattern. These designs of wide rectangles are for the wall, but you can add more repeats to size them for bed quilts.

◇ How to Add or Subtract Leaf Units

There are several ways to add or subtract a leaf to or from a flower block. The easiest method is to add a separate leaf block to the quilt. *Waving Poppies* in chapter 6 adds a leaf block to accompany a poppy, which has no foliage. Or leafless flowers can be inserted into the lattice work of *Leafy Bower* and will, by association, gain the impression of owning some greenery. Another method is to add rows of units to the flower and draw a leaf arrangement. Figure 29a adds one row of units to the bottom and one side of the *Poppy* block. The leaves are attached to the calyx, or base, of the flower. Now the block consists of 3 x 3 units with the leaves included. (The drawing is only to see the style. Enlarging the drawing to a full-sized block is not necessary because the same equation of chapter 3, page 21 still applies.) In figure 29b the same two rows of units are added, but this new poppy has three leaves and a stem. You can subtly shade the different leaves by choosing a second fabric for the leaf tucked behind another.

With the *Posy* pattern, add rows of units in the same manner as above for an interesting off-center arrangement (fig. 30b). Now the block is a square of 5 x 5 units. Figure 30c shows leaves symmetrically placed at each indention of petals, but the block has become rectangular and can be used horizontally or vertically. A less elongated rectangle is formed by adding only one row of units to the bottom of the posy (fig. 30d). By borrowing the blank unit in the lower left corner of the original block, a leaf is extended into the new bottom row. How? The two blank units (one borrowed and one from the added row) are cut into the A and B curves. Two B patches form the main leaf. In the two adjacent units to the right, the same method creates a leaf partially hidden by the flower. An A patch and a B patch make this leaf.

But, you say, that's back to dealing with a long rectangle instead of a symmetrical square design. Except for the square quilt for a king-size bed, we most often require a quilt longer than wide. As discussed earlier, the long rectangle helps lengthen a quilt design. If adding that extra row of units to each *Posy* block (fig. 30d) makes the quilt too long, try the elongated block only at the top and bottom of the quilt (fig. 31). Note that units "borrowed" from the side blocks to add more leaves create a border effect without increasing the width of the quilt.

It is even easier to subtract leaves from a flower. *Tulip #1* in figure 32 is 5 x 5 units. By removing the row of units on the left side and the row across the

Fig. 29. Addition of leaves to the *Poppy* by adding a row of units to one side and to the bottom.

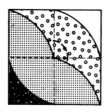

Original *Poppy* block.

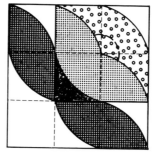

a. Two leaves attached to base of flower.

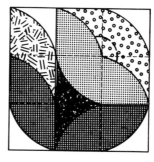

b. Three leaves and stem extension.

bottom, the flower is reduced to a block of 4 x 4 units. This frees the design so that it may be combined with other 4 x 4 flower blocks or developed in any way that occurs to you.

◇ The Borders and Their Modules

You will discover a number of designs in the borders that are not illustrated elsewhere. In chapter 5 there are various shapes of leaves, ribbons, bows, hearts, shells, etc. These designs can be separated into blocks and used as independent patterns. Using the ¼" scale on the Block Marker as discussed in chapter 1, place the marker over the border design. This will help you isolate the number of units needed to assemble just one heart or leaf.

Calculate the dimensions of a border using the

118

Fig. 30. Rows added to *Posy*. Patches "borrowed" to complete leaves.

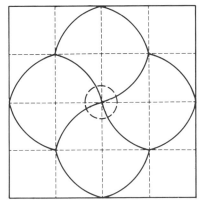

a. Original block.

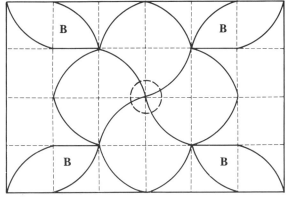

c. Row added to 2 sides.

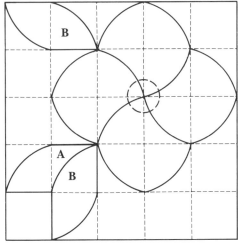

b. Row added to one side and bottom.

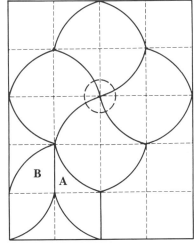

d. One row added to bottom.

same technique that was discussed in chapter 3; that is, use the number of units in the design, across or down, to determine the size of templates. The technique for assembling the modules of a border is also the same as for a flower block, by horizontal or vertical rows. What differs is the fact that a flower block is one module and a border may have several different shapes. For this reason I tend to use the term "module" when I talk about the borders. It's only a matter of identifying the modules with the aid of the Block Marker. Logic will tell you whether it's easier to assemble by squares, rectangles, long strips or by a combination of these. Let's examine the breakdown of one border as an example.

Figure 33 cuts up the border *Rosebud Panel #2* into modules. What I call spacing bands are really un-

pieced, separate borders on either side of the patchwork. The Block Marker will tell you that, from the corner to the center, the length of the spacing band next to the body of the quilt is equivalent to 11 square units, and the outside one is 14 square units (not counting seam allowances). These bands, however, have no patchwork and can be cut as whole strips. If you do not need center seams, double the length of the strips. They are illustrated with mitered corners.

Between these spacing bands is the patchwork border. Notice that the corner is assembled as a 2 x 2 unit block. The leaf of the corner bud (the other leaf for the bud is not shown but will be around the corner) is assembled as a separate module. Next come two rows of blank units, or spacing rows. No patchwork here, so cut one piece equal to 2 units wide

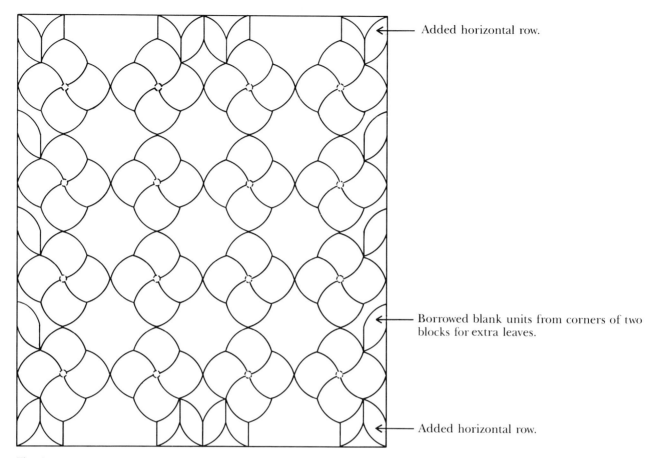

Added horizontal row.

Borrowed blank units from corners of two blocks for extra leaves.

Added horizontal row.

Fig. 31. Extended *Posy* blocks are top and bottom rows.

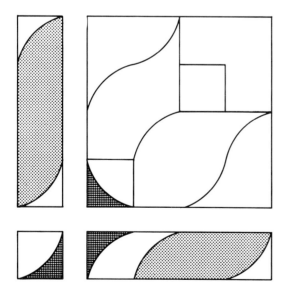

Fig. 32. Reduce a block by removing the leaf and stem units. Replace the flower base with background patch.

120

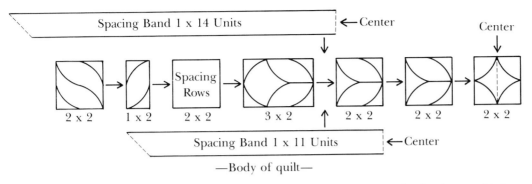

Fig. 33. Border divided into assembly modules. Centers will match when border is assembled.

by 2 units long. The remaining modules are assembled similarly. Several combination patches can be cut in these units, such as whole leaves and the rounded top of the horizontal bud. For another example of a border broken down into modules, see the assembly diagram for the border of *Dutch Bulbs*, chapter 6.

I have drawn the borders with the idea that all corners are assembled as blocks. They may not always look like independent designs, but they are treated as such. (For the one exception, *Ribbon Twist*, see the assembly diagram for *Woodland Favorites*, chapter 6.)

Although the border of figure 33 has fabric strips or bands on each side, many others do not. Generally, the patchwork borders benefit from additions of these spacing bands. The separation of the curved patches of the border from the main body of the quilt isolates each and gives a respite from the movement of the curves. Adding bands, remember, will increase the dimensions of your quilt.

You may want to try some curved patchwork without investing a great deal of time. Not all quilts need borders, particularly contemporary styles. Or you may simply prefer wide bands where you can do some special quilting. Another time-saver is to use borders of mitered stripes. The long, straight lines of color can be a good foil for the curved patchwork. In the fabric shops you can find muted or floral stripes as well as regimental ones to blend with your quilt's style.

◇ Consideration of Scale

We all know that the dimensions of a quilt must be reckoned with, but let's remember there is more than one way to do the reckoning. Multiplying a block size by a number of repeats to establish a quilt's measurements is not the only way; it's merely one way. It's so easy to calculate the size of a repeated block quilt that I think sometimes we fall into the habit of choosing only patterns that will make a "nice medium-sized block." Because the curved patterns must be scaled to a specific size, I worry that some will be labeled without further consideration as too large or too small. Don't dismiss the 2 x 2 or 3 x 3 unit flower as insignificant. Because they have fewer units, they are the best choices for the larger templates. On the other hand, the use of large flowers in a repeated block design may not be appealing, but a single floral medallion is.

The scale of the patterns will influence the style of your quilt. Large, quickly pieced flowers are not as compatible with a traditional style as with a contemporary design. On the other hand, smaller flowers that appear delicate will not produce a bold, modern quilt.

To add subtlety to your quilt, experiment with a combination of flowers that have varying numbers of units but are still of one scale. Or try one flower in more than one scale. Another idea is to patch the main body of the quilt in one scale and the border in another scale. Sometimes this method improves a quilt's proportions. (See *The Power of the Pansy* by Susan Croft, page 34.) With consideration of scale and dimensions in mind, look through the quilts in chapter 6 again. Read about the use of a transparent overlay to change the scale (p. 81).

◇ Choosing the Quilting Design

Have you thought how you are going to quilt your choice of blocks? Many of the styles will call for some innovative quilting, particularly a repeated block that has minimum background space. Although the flowers can be outlined, you will probably want to find ways to add more than a single line around each petal. The hood of the *Jack-in-the-Pulpit* would seem more curved and recessed with waves of quilting echoing the curves of the patches. The *Bluet* might have miniature clamshell quilting in its center. Meander quilting or stippling would also engrave flower centers. Have you considered using lines of back-

Fig. 34. Straight-line quilting can be used in certain petals.

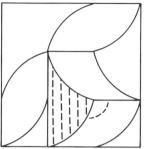

a. To suggest a shaded side.

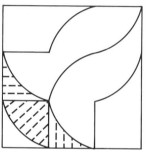

b. For a perception of depth.

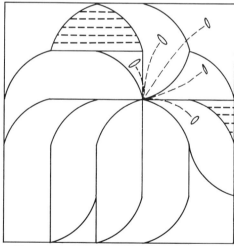

c. To recess the underside of petals.

stitch quilting with silk-twist instead of embroidery for stamens? And, of course, it's natural to add veins to texture the leaves. For traditionalists, *Leafy Bower*, without flowers added to the blocks, offers some room for quilted wreaths, feathers or bouquets.

The rule of thumb for quilting patchwork of straight-line geometrics is to use curves somewhere to soften those lines. With the Curved Two-Patch System, the opposite applies—relieve the curves somewhere with straight-line quilting. This can be planned for the background, borders or certain flower petals, and such lines should be carefully thought out. There are petals, such as in the *Bell Blossom* and *Morning Glory*, that suggest a side of the flower turned away from the light and that can receive straight quilted lines (fig. 34a). The inside of the *Bluebonnet* (fig. 34b) can be recessed with straight lines. The same type of quilting will shade the underside of petals of the *Roadside Lily* (fig. 34c). Notice that the quilting lines are kept parallel to an adjacent straight line of a patch or they are perpendicular to a curved edge.

For quilting the background of blocks, consider simple parallel lines. Cross-hatching, diamonds or a basket weave are other common background fillers. Browse through your reference books for quilting styles. There is one danger, however, to be aware of: Different quilting designs coming together at oblique angles can meet in a blur. The change, such as from background to leaf, should be quite pronounced. This change can be in direction, density or both.

Whether you want to quilt within flower petals or in the background of the blocks, I recommend that you have a basic plan in mind before cutting the patches. Obviously a petal cut with 2″ templates will not have much open space for quilting. So study the pattern to find what combination patches you can cut. Your quilting will be easier if you avoid crossing too many seam lines.

Plain bands for borders are good areas to echo the curves of the patchwork. Encase the curved quilting in the bands with some straight lines to maintain separation from the curved patchwork. Then such designs as cable or rope quilting are appropriate for the middle of the bands.

◇ Fabric Choices

Calicoes, geometrics, splashy nondescript prints, and muted or clear solids will impose their own personalities on your style of quilt. Your choice of fabric and colors will help define your quilt as romantic, tailored, country, contemporary or exotic. That is in the realm of personal preferences. I've limited myself to how to use different fabrics with the curved patches.

In chapter 3, I talked about the advantages and

disadvantages of solid colors. I briefly mentioned that the A and B templates can be used without worry of reversals on many calicoes, but not on directional fabrics. This is not to suggest you eliminate all geometric prints, but to caution you about them. They will complicate your work with curves because you must remember to reverse the templates, but such fabrics often add zest. If you want to experiment with such a fabric, use the same guidelines as for straight-line quilting. You don't want to take the bend out of a leaf or straighten the curve of a petal. So straight lines, whether in quilting or regimental prints, should be lined up with a straight edge of a patch or be perpendicular to the curved edge. Look at figure 34 again and think of those lines as stripes in a fabric rather than quilting stitches. The effect is the same.

The same guidelines extend also to the use of directional fabric in the background of blocks and in borders. Naturally, the straight grain of the fabric helps in lining up these prints. Remember, though, that they must be matched with adjacent patches, stripe to stripe, row of dots to row of dots, ad infinitum! Maybe a wiser spot for the use of geometric prints would be a leaf cut from a combination template, a petal of one patch or spacing bands that separate the patchwork of the quilt and the border.

. . . How Does Your Garden Grow?, 32″ x 62″, a variation made by Linda Halpin. Patchwork with appliquéd stems. The *Strawberry Skirt* by Nancy Drum, hand-appliquéd and embroidered. The machine-appli-quéd elbow patches on the sweater are of leather, velvet and corduroy. All items were designed by author and are shown on a flannel grid sheet used to lay out patches.

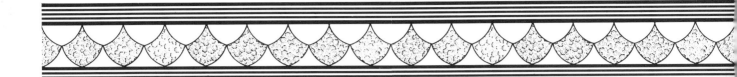

CHAPTER 8

Freeing the Patterns for Appliqué

Previously there has been little reason to interpret a patchwork pattern for appliqué. Those of you who prefer appliqué like to work with curved pieces. More often than not, you also like representational shapes. You have had an enviable advantage. Patterns of naturalized plant life belong almost exclusively to appliqué. The more I work with the A and B curves, the more I realize they are as useful to one who works with appliqué as to the patchworker. At first I was excited about offering the opportunity to make realistic flowers only to those who piece rather than apply patches. But in developing the Curved Two-Patch System, I came to several conclusions. One flower might be easy to draw upright, but not diagonally, and vice versa. Stems appear so fat—unless I add more rules to the system—that I eliminated most of them. Some flowers have too many units to be used as repeated blocks unless a miniature scale is used. Whenever I felt restricted, I thought, "I could do that in appliqué."

Probably because I am primarily a patchworker, that thought had to present itself repeatedly before I realized that there is something here for appliqué people. You are free to lift the flowers from patchwork and embellish them. You can add narrow bias strips for stems. You can group flowers of different proportions, overlap or scatter them. You can make subtle changes in positioning a flower or leaf. You can even curve a series of leaves into a wreath.

The system also offers you the same advantage for appliqué that it does to patchworkers—a simple method for calculating the dimensions of an entire series of designs. You use the same method for determining the size of your patterns that is used for patchwork (chapter 3, "Template Size Determines Block Measurement"). Figure 11 and "How to Draw Templates" tell you how to make any size template. If you are planning to use small templates, you may want to experiment with drawing a deeper arc. Then compare patterns drawn with the template of the Curved Two-Patch System and with your new one.

◇ Drawing Templates for Appliqué

It's at this point that you separate from the patchworker, who uses the A and B curved templates to cut a number of patches and sews them together to form a petal. You will use the A and B templates to trace the outline of an entire petal. Then you make a new template of this tracing for appliqué.

Let's use the *Cabbage Rose* as an example and assume you want to make a pillow top that is 12″ x 12″. The rose consists of 6 x 6 units (fig. 35a). Use 1½″ templates to make a rose 9″ x 9″. This size of flower can be appliquéd to a 12″ pillow top with 1½″ background showing on all sides. Trace and cut the 1½″ templates, the square plus the A and B curves. (See the sheet of templates at the end of chapter 3.) Use these templates to draw the appliqué patterns.

To draw the appliqué patterns, you need a sheet of professional quality graph paper. Unfortunately the cheaper grade for students is not accurate enough. Unless you can buy extra large sheets, yours is the standard size, 8½″ x 11″. Make a new grid on the sheet by marking as many 1½″ squares as possible in the width and length. You can draw more than enough units for the rose from the length, but only five units across. This is not a problem because one petal can be superimposed on another to draw a pattern. Refer to the original design to see how the rose is broken down into square units. Reproduce the outline of the petals and leaves with the three patchwork templates.

In figure 35b, notice that only certain edges of the templates are traced. They turn in all directions to present a curve or straight edge for a petal. Simply line up the other edges of the template on the drawn

Fig. 35. Use patchwork templates to draw patterns for appliqué.

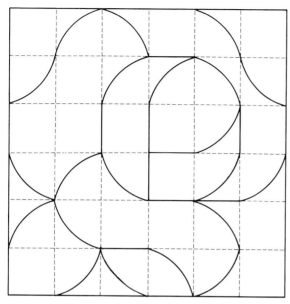

a. Original *Cabbage Rose.*

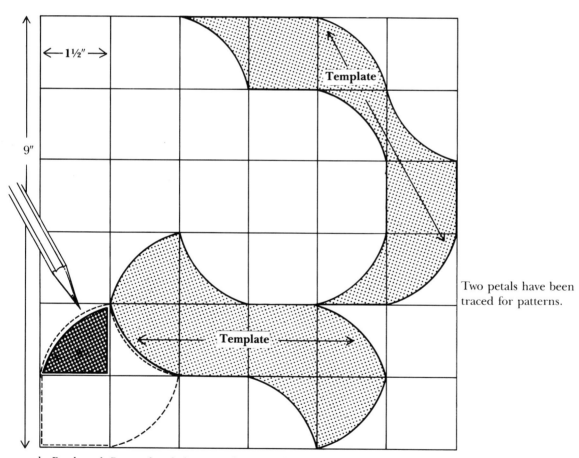

1½″

9″

Template

Template

Template

Two petals have been
traced for patterns.

b. Patchwork B template being traced to complete a leaf pattern.

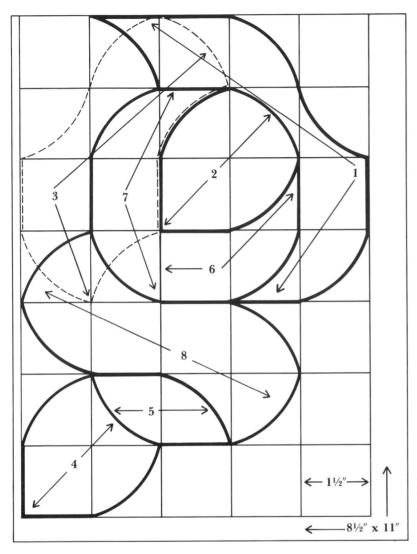

Fig. 36. Graph paper with 1½″ grid drawn. Full-sized appliqué patterns drawn. Petal no. 3 is superimposed with dash lines. Leaf no. 4 is repositioned to fit the grid sheet.

← 1½″ →

← 8½″ x 11″

grid lines. Figure 36 illustrates one way to fit all the patterns on a single grid sheet. It isn't necessary to trace all the petals in the order they appear in the original drawing, but if you find it confusing to have extra lines overlapping the patterns, use a second sheet of graph paper. Take care to faithfully follow the original for each pattern. Now trace each pattern onto template material and cut. You may want to make a simple tracing of the flower diagram, mark each petal and leaf with a number and mark the full-sized templates similarly. This is for easy identification of the odd-shaped templates.

◇ Conventional Appliqué Procedure

From here you proceed as with any appliqué project. Always the first step is to preshrink and press your fabrics. Mark patterns on the right side of the fabric

and remember to add seam allowances before cutting. Notice that these flower patterns eliminate many of the troublesome inside points, which are difficult to turn under, and that many raw edges can be overlapped with another appliqué.

Finally, you need to decide upon an order of assembly. Using the *Cabbage Rose* example, figure 37 suggests one plan. By the time the eighth petal is applied, all raw edges are covered. This last petal will have all its seam allowances turned under.

Mark on the background material (the 12″ square plus seam allowances) the center and perimeter of the 9″ square into which the rose will be applied. Inconspicuous pencil dots are sufficient. Some fabrics will leave a strong enough impression if the outline of the 9″ square is pressed with an iron. Prepare each appliqué by gluing or basting under the seam allow-

127

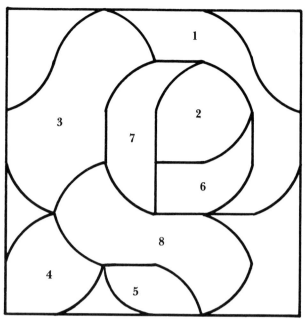

Fig. 37. Order of appliqué assembly to take advantage of overlapping raw edges.

ances that will not be overlapped. Clip any excess bubble or folds in the turn-under. Then I suggest that you lay out all pieces on the background to make sure the patterns are accurate and that the assembly order is logical. Remove all except number one, and baste it to the background by your preferred method—thread or glue stick. If you use the latter, do so sparingly because it tends to flatten the appliqué, so much so that even outline quilting will fail to puff it up again. Now you're ready to appliqué.

Having read through the steps of the appliqué process for the *Cabbage Rose*, you might ask, "What's so different about it?" Only one step, enlarging the design. There is no call for freehand drawing to draft the patterns. You may have no difficulty with freehand drawing, but I think the owner of an untrained hand pales at the thought. When guidelines are removed, the hand doesn't spring into free-form design. It's frozen motionless. So having the templates of the Curved Two-Patch System do the drawing will be of merit to many.

◇ **An Exercise: Adapting Patterns for Appliqué**

Figure 38 shows the *Cabbage Rose* with more adaptations for appliqué. My idea was to make an off-center arrangement. I outlined the rose on tracing paper and omitted the two large leaves. To show that the rose was the only mature one on a living bush, I wanted tender sprays of a bud and leaves to peek out

around the sides. Next I curved lines under the petals to indicate bias stems. Because the new leaves would not belong to the large rose, I made them in two smaller scales. On graph paper using a scale one-half that of the *Cabbage Rose*, I drew the *Bud With Stem #2* (page 44), but I left out the leaves and base and chose only the bud portion of the design. I also drew a leaf form in the same scale. For more variation, I drew a second leaf that was three-quarters of the rose's scale. Once I placed the tracing of the rose on top of the three graphed designs, it was simply a matter of twisting and turning the tracing paper until each design element underneath was gracefully positioned on the bias lines. A final tracing of the additions gave me a completed diagram of how the appliqué would look. Moreover, I had the drawings in the appropriate scales. Of course you can work directly on the background fabric to find a pleasing arrangement. The paper exercise, however, was visually helpful in deciding dimensions. The only freehand drawing was a curved line for the bias strips! I hope this is not only an exercise that will help you design your own appliqué but also one that will be fun. You have so much freedom with appliqué that it's a pity to be dependent upon patterns without being able to personalize them.

An excellent choice for appliqué is *Basket of Blooms* (p. 52), one of the flower designs. Experiment by using tracing paper. Because you can lift the flowers and leaves from patchwork, you may find a softer arrangement. Another likely candidate for modification is the quilt design *Cornered daisy* (chapter 6). Several large flowers can substitute for the daisy. You might want to use a twist of ribbons in place of the bands of leaves.

The group of borders and quilt designs should suggest many ideas. The diagram of the *Pennsylvania Dutch Crib Quilt* was developed for patchwork, but Eulalia Frenzel made a rendition, *Blue Hearts*, in appliqué. See page 34. The design wasn't changed, only the piecing technique.

Study the photos of appliquéd projects for ideas. Eulalia, whose specialty is quilted bell pulls, used small-scale flowers for the photographed sample (page 71). From my diagram, she expertly interpreted the vines that I had drawn freehand. Nancy Drum enjoys working with miniatures. For an A-line skirt (page 124), she appliquéd a band of leaves and two sizes of strawberries. Note that she used embroidery for the miniature concave curve of the stems. (Until I talked her out if it, she was using a scale one-half that size.) The problem of circling the design around a tapering A-line was solved by omitting one of the smaller berries at each side seam.

One of my first projects with this system was the

Fig. 38. Smaller scale additions to *Cabbage Rose* appliqué.

pair of elbow patches for a worn but favorite sweater (page 124). The patches make a quick project for those who do machine appliqué. This is one project that can make use of scraps of velvet, corduroy and wool. However, hand stitching the elbow patches to the sleeves takes a bit longer. The *Stained-glass Rose* (page 71) is a combination of methods. First I patched the curved design and then appliquéd the black lead lines.

This chapter is brief because drawing the appliqué templates is the only new technique to explain. The designs are the same for everyone. Whether to do them in patches, appliqué or both is your choice.

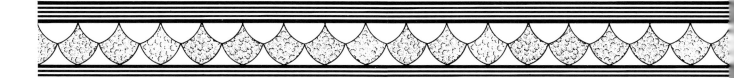

Index of Block Designs by Number of Units

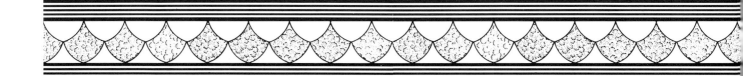

Index of Blocks, Borders and Quilt Designs